Happy Cooking
Nick Price

nick's warehouse cookbook

the accidental chef

nick price

cookery collaborator jenny mc crea
illustrations danielle morgan
photographs dermott dunbar

BOOKLINK

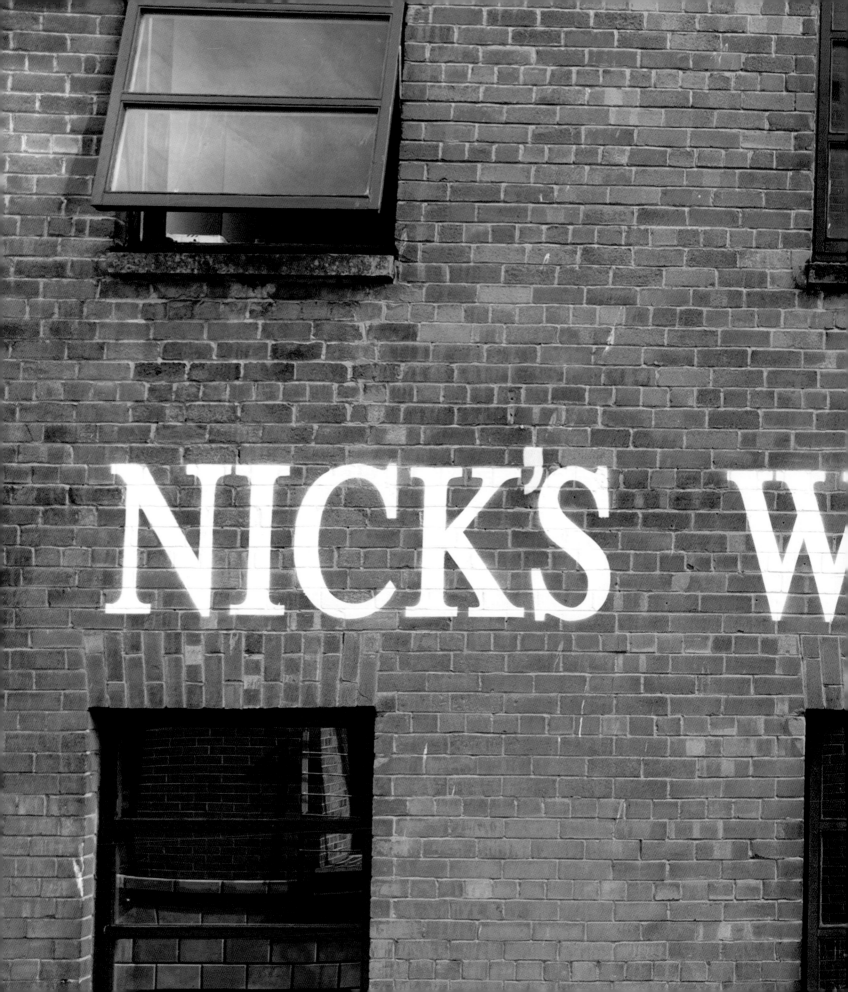

contents

Introduction

Why the 'Accidental Chef' I hear you ask? Well, I didn't set out to be a chef, I wanted to be a manager, as it appeared to me back then that they just swanned about all day and did very little. Of course I later learnt the error of my assumptions!

I trained at Bournemouth College and managed to obtain an OND in Hotel and Catering Operations. Fortunately, this course believed in teaching the classical basics of cookery along with front of house management. We were taught by people who had worked in the Savoy, Claridges and the Caprice. Our Restaurant Lecturer was a former Chief Steward of B.O.A.C. (Yes, it was that long ago!)

This meant that when I left college I could cook but chose to go into management, from a Hard Rock style Burger Bar/Disco to a Wine Bar with a few in between which we won't talk about.

Gordon Street, 1988

Kilmood before renovation

One day in the Wine Bar the chef didn't turn in and I covered his shift. It was all down hill from there – I was now cooking for a living. I learned as I went but luckily the classical way of doing things had been imbedded in my brain and even now I find myself using techniques I was taught at the age of eighteen.

Daft Eddy's was the start of my cooking career in Northern Ireland, unless you count a few summers back in the days of the Peppermill in Holywood with Teddy and Brenda Fix. I had five years at Daft Eddy's, then five years at Nick's Restaurant in Kilmood and now twenty years at Nick's Warehouse in Belfast … how did it all happen?

In 1988, Hill Street was a desolate place of run down warehouses, sack merchants, derelict buildings and its saving grace, cobbled streets. We had been looking for a site in Belfast for about a year as we had a dream of opening a proper wine bar in the city. We had mentioned this to a friend, Morris Crawford, who was working on Barrie Todd's building in Hill Street. He suggested that Barrie might like to sell off 35–39 Hill Street, next door to his new offices. We were presented with four walls and a pigeon guano depository. I am not renowned for my visualisation skills and this was nearly a bridge too far.

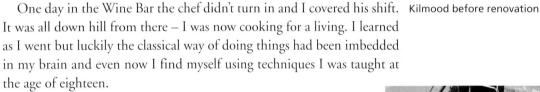

Hill Street frontage, 1989

However, there was a carrot dangled before us in the form of an Urban Development Grant and suddenly we were the proud but slightly shell-shocked owners of an embryo wine bar.

Work in progress, 1989

Ben and Adam

We engaged Todds as the architects and Downhill Construction as the contractors. We then had to buy a pub licence. We discovered one for a pub in Tomb Street which was about to be demolished to make way for the new motorway and rail link. This was the easy bit as we soon found out. The hurdles we had to jump nearly did for us and you would hardly believe them today but we succeeded, big thank you to my mum for believing in us.

The refurb took a while as we only had four walls and a sort of roof. We needed to put in 3 floors and a new roof. We eventually said goodbye to the pigeons, told the contractors we were moving in, ready or not and opened the doors for the first time on 6th December 1989.

Man looks at menu and says, 'what's this venison?' 'It's deer', the waitress replies.
'I don't care how much it is, I can afford it', replies the customer.

This was a huge project for us and we needed some help on all fronts, so we advertised for 'An Amazing Person' as we knew it was going to take someone special with a sense of humour and a 'can do' attitude to get us going.

We found our amazing person going by the name of Martin Edwards. He had become disillusioned with teaching and was after a change – and my goodness did he get one! He was possibly as eccentric as me so he fitted right in.

The first floor under construction

So I cooked and Kathy did everything else. Our two sons were quite young but managed to cope with their parents' busy lifestyle although we still feel guilty for the lack of any kind of normality in their lives. But come four o'clock in the afternoon the boys were to be found in the kitchen scrounging something nice from the pastry chef, and our resident guard dog, Biskit, was demanding to be released from the office to hold court in the wine bar. She was an amazing little dog with a personality bigger than all of us. Think Chalky and Rick Stein and you have the picture.

Biskit

Boredom did set in sometimes and one day Adam and Ben chanced upon a tray of eggs and were overcome by an incredible urge to throw them from the top floor windows … Martin, bless him, dealt with the fall out and the boys were set to write an essay on the cause and effects of gravity.

The consensus of opinion when we moved to Hill Street was that Nick and Kathy were either 'Very Courageous' or 'Had Lost the Plot Completely'. The truth lies somewhere in the middle. We couldn't afford to do this without the grant and the grant was only available in Hill Street, part of Northside Development Area as it was known then, the Cathedral Quarter as is now.

Martin Edwards

More work!

Northside had a champion in the form of Richard Needham, Secretary of State. His enthusiasm and drive made things happen, for which we were very grateful.

A lot of our lovely customers from Kilmood days worked in town and, bless them, they all beat a path to our door. In the early 90s it was still acceptable to have a civilised lunch. Many customers claimed that they did more business on the way to their table at Nick's than they did at them. I blame the Americans for the loss of a great Irish institution – you can only drink so much fizzy water before you drown you know!

1991 was a great summer due to the first visit of the Tall Ships. An amazing hot summer. Who would have thought that a bunch of beautiful old sailing ships could do so much for a city which had suffered enough. We didn't stop that summer and the wave of enthusiasm carried us all the way to Christmas.

A big vote of thanks to the guys who had the vision and organised it for us.

We had a calamity in 1992. Kathy and I were away skiing and we suffered a fire on the top floor of the restaurant.

The original wine bar

Someone had left an iron on. The top two floors of the restaurant were out of action and there was a lot of smoke damage. It was like a blow to the head but Kathy said we would be back in business in ten days and by golly we were. Bruised but not beaten. The top two floors were back in action three months later. This was when we decided to open at night time for dinner to recoup our losses from the fire. Our finances were strained and it could have been a lot worse but for the support and kindness of our suppliers. They rallied round to a man – 'Pay us when you can', they said. Needless to say we did and a lot of them are still with us. Thank you.

We apparently weathered a recession in these years as well but we were so small and working so hard that we didn't notice. Certainly nothing like our experiences at the moment.

Time has moved on and over the years we have employed a great number of wonderful people who have all been part of the reason for our success. We have learned something from everyone who has worked for us. Some came as youngsters and left as adults, the transformations being incredible. Some who you thought would never make it turned out to be superstars. Some came for a summer job and stayed five years. All we know is that we are incredibly grateful to have had the pleasure of working with you. You know who you are – take a bow.

Customer gets a bit 'fresh' with one of the waiting staff, "don't touch what you can't afford", she says. Quick as a flash the customer replies that he is willing to save up.

New girl student waitress first day working goes up to a table and engages in conversation with customers. Asked what she is studying she replies drama.
Customer comments,'oh you are a bit of a thespian'. Girl bursts into tears runs out through the door never to be seen again.

The original layout of the first floor restaurant

Nick's Warehouse has always been on 'neutral turf' at the heart of the city and has therefore played host to all and sundry – our only stipulation being that they paid their bill and had a good time. We are reliably informed by Jim McDowell that on one day in particular we had members of Sinn Fein in one corner, members of the UDA in another and the Chief Constable upstairs in the Restaurant. Of course we were completely oblivious to this, apart from the Chief Constable that is.

Ok, so I love Burgundy ...

We received a lovely letter from the late Mo Mowlam thanking us for the use of the wine bar as her office during her time as Shadow Secretary of State for Northern Ireland, whilst she got to know all the movers and shakers. Sadly we never saw her once the Labour Party got into power.

In the middle of 1996, we were very busy and felt we needed to expand. We persuaded our neighbour Barrie Todd that he didn't really need a car park on the ground floor of his building and that he would be a lot better off letting it to us ... to our horror he agreed and even worse the bank said yes to the loan we asked for. I remember sitting in the Managers office of the Ulster Bank in Waring St, now better known as the Private Bar off the Great Room of The Merchant Hotel.

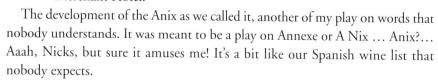

Lovely Polish waitress is asked if salmon is wild or farmed; 'it is domesticated', she replied.

Kathy

The development of the Anix as we called it, another of my play on words that nobody understands. It was meant to be a play on Annexe or A Nix ... Anix?... Aaah, Nicks, but sure it amuses me! It's a bit like our Spanish wine list that nobody expects.

As the Anix was on the same level we could develop it without disturbing the winebar and then one weekend in November 1997 our very long suffering contractor Joe Tomelty and his team from Lough Construction knocked it through and got it up and running for Christmas ... running being the operative word as we had trebled the size of the restaurant.

We could suddenly seat 130 on the ground floor and 50 on the first floor so we had to grow up very fast and had to build structures and systemise everything as we knew it wouldn't work any other way. To this day new starts sometimes comment on how organised we are with all our checklists and systems.

They say that for every action there is an opposite and equal reaction and having a lot more space downstairs meant that the upstairs restaurant was not as busy and anyway people were looking for a more simple lunch, leaving the upstairs for special or important occasions.

Wine bar revamped

But then that opens up other opportunities and we have a great intimate space to offer for meetings, product launches weddings, etc.

Time has moved on and from being the only occupants of the now named Cathedral Quarter we are slap bang in the middle of Belfast's most happening area and a lot more competition, but that's good for us and keeps us on our toes!

Somewhere in the middle of all the mayhem of the last twenty years I found time to do various TV shows, the notable ones being Pot Luck for RTÉ (a sort of 'Ready Steady Cook' with a bingo caller) for two series, they actually asked me back and I was lucky enough to be included in a show called '10 of the Best' (no it was a cookery show). Which put me in the very exalted company of people like Derry Clarke of L'Écrivain in Dublin and Paul Flynn of, The Tannery in Dungarvan, and the northern element was of course Paul Rankin and the late Robbie Millar, who is greatly missed.

I loved doing these shows as in reality I am a frustrated actor going back to the age of twelve when I appeared in a production of A Midsummer Nights Dream but to give you the level, I was the Wall in the Mechanicals play within the play !

I hope you enjoy this book. It has been hard work to write and very good discipline for me. Thank you for coming to our restaurants, some of you ever since Daft Eddy days. We couldn't have done it without you!

> Strangest request …. recently one of our waitresses was asked to go with a lady customer to help her apply fake tan in the washrooms; she didn't even leave a tip!

> Two little old ladies came in one day and ordered a bottle of German wine which we served them. After about two minutes, they called the waiter over, pointed at the vintage date and said they couldn't drink it as it was past its sell by date … what can you say?

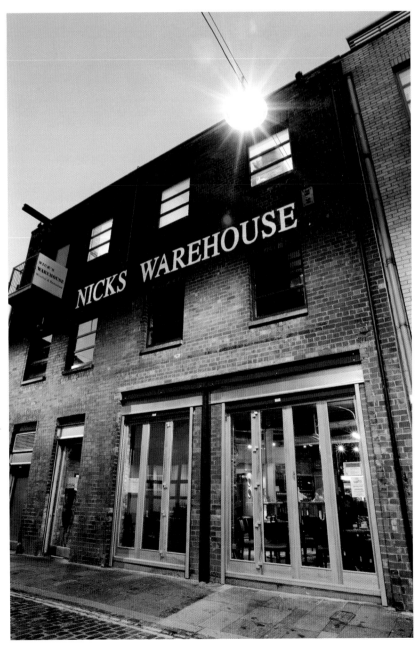

batterie de cuisine
or a list of kit you may find useful if setting up a kitchen

Knives as good as you can afford at very least 3 of different sizes

A good sharpening steel

Potato peeler: I like the u-shaped swiss ones

A good heavy iron pan

Stainless steel saucepans – various sizes

Measuring jug

Chopping board: a good heavy wooden one

Pressure cooker [not essential and a bit scary but modern ones are great]

Electronic scales

Citrus juicer manual or electric

Hand held liquidiser

Pestle and mortar [for really heavy granite ones try the Asian supermarket]

Flour sieve

Colander

Fish slice

Ladles

Liquidiser

Piping bag and nozzles

Potato ricer

Digital thermometer

Mandolin for slicing

Blowtorch

Dariole moulds for Pannacottas and little summer puddings

A lot of these items are available from proper catering suppliers such as AJ Stuart in Belfast or www.nisbets.co.uk online, and the Asian Supermarket on the Ormeau Rd, Belfast, has some wonderful things like steamers and choppers at the back of the shop.

store cupboard

Noodles

Dried pasta

Coconut milk

Thai green curry paste

Oils – olive, sunflower, sesame

Tinned anchovies

Trifle sponges

Rice – aborio, basmati, long grain, pudding

Sugar – caster, soft brown, Demerara

Lentils – green, red, puy

Raisins – sultanas, dried apricots

Flours – self raising, plain, strong bread, sauce flour

Tins – sweetcorn, tuna, plums, tomatoes, chopped

Stock cubes or powders – chicken, beef, veggie

Mustards – English, grain mustard, Dijon

Chilli sauce

Tomato ketchup

Worcester sauce

Vinegars – cider, wine red and white, balsamic, sherry etc.

Peanut butter

Dessicated coconut

Salt, sea salt, kosher salt is also great but hard to get here

Spices – cayenne, 5 spice, coriander seeds, cumin seeds, fennel seeds, yellow mustard seeds,chilli flakes, pimenton

Thickening agents – cornflour, potato flour, McDougalls thickening granules

Ketjap Manis – Indonesian soy sauce

Curry pastes [different heats, Pataks are good]

Mango chutney

Gravy browning

Golden syrup

Cocoa powder

Drinking chocolate

Baking powder

Bicarbonate of soda

Cream of tartar

Porridge oats

Fish sauce [Thai]

Nuts pecan, hazelnut, cashew, brazils

Freezer – breads, pitta, French stick

the wine story

Kathy and I are passionate about wine and have always considered it an important part of the restaurant business. We have made it our mission to buy new and interesting wines for our customers that are also great value for money.

So when four or five years ago Maxine and Brian Nelson discussed the possibility of setting up a wine company to sell to the trade and private individuals there was only one answer. We now wholesale to about seventy trade customers and retail through **www.nickswines.co.uk** as we hold the full on/off licence.

The truth of the matter is that Maxine does all the work ably assisted by her wee team and we provide the public face and host the wine tastings. And as nothing gets on the list unless it has been tasted and approved by our 'Tasting Panel' (that's 6 people with very differing tastes) we also have to taste a lot of wine! Which sounds fun but when faced with thirty or forty wines to assess can be a grim task, especially when only three or four make the grade.

The future? We aspire to a retail wine shop and the enthusiasm that exists throughout our little company will definitely get us there. Watch this space.

Oh – and log onto **www.nickswines.co.uk**!

www.nickswines.co.uk

breads

Bread was for a long time a bit of a mystery to me. I was a little afraid of it and thought that if we started making it we wouldn't have time left for other jobs in the kitchen; but with some reliable recipes and good advice we mastered it and now everyone in the kitchen is able to do it.

We make three kinds of bread each day: always our wheaten scones – or as Norman Beggs calls them 'our rock cakes'. Just think of all that good roughage you are missing out on Norman! – then we make a white yeast bread often flavoured with different things, and finally a brown bread; usually a wholemeal, but sometimes a rye flour blended with strong white flour to give lightness. Often we put in all sorts of seeds as it gives a lovely nutty texture.

Anyway, recipes …

White bread

1kg strong white flour
20g yeast fresh or dried (1x7 g =15g fresh)
3 tsp salt
3 tblsp oil
750ml water at blood heat
egg wash – 200ml milk and 1 egg beaten to glaze

In a large bowl, or machine bowl if doing it mechanically, combine all the dry ingredients. If using the easy blend dried yeast it goes in now, plus any flavouring you fancy. See the suggestions listed below. If using fresh yeast, mix it up with the water. If doing it by hand gradually incorporate all the liquid and the oil.

Work the dough, kneading it either by hand or in a mixer bowl for at least 5 mins. This develops the gluten and helps the rise. You can leave it in the machine longer, but you will be getting tired if kneading it by hand, so place in a bowl and cover with a damp cloth.

Leave to rise in a warm place for an hour. It should at least double in size. The oven needs to be at 185°C.

Now knock back the dough and put into either oiled and floured loaf tins or make up into little rolls. Allow to rise for about 30 mins and then egg wash and bake rolls for 20 mins, loaves for 35 mins, or until the rolls/loaves sound hollow when tapped on the bottom. Cool on a wire rack.

Flavourings: cheese, onion, mixed herbs, rosemary and raisins, tomato and garlic, sundried tomato, pesto, cumin seeds, fennel seeds, nuts various.

sundried tomato bread

Ulster has a great baking tradition, and we try to embrace it in what we bake in the Warehouse to the extent that our 'petits fours' were described by an eminent churchman as being a little Presbyterian. What he meant was that they were not too far removed from tray bakes and 'wee buns'.

The next few recipes are from my friend and food hero Robert Ditty, a master baker from Castledawson, who has taught me to make the lightest soda farls and breads that I have ever tasted. Of course, baking is a science as well as an art, so you have to measure stuff! You will note he uses self raising flour. He has discovered that the millers take more care of the process when milling this and it works better. I have to say I agree, having tasted these and his other breads, it also doesn't have that heavy soda taste.

Robert Ditty's soda farls cooked on the griddle

makes 8 farls

450g self raising flour
pinch salt
2 tblsp vegetable oil
420/450ml buttermilk

Preheat a heavy based griddle or pan. Dust with a little flour and when the flour starts to colour, reduce the heat slightly and it is ready to bake.

Sift the flour and salt at least twice as this aerates the flour and gives a lighter product. Make a well in the middle and add the oil and buttermilk.

Bring the mix together with a spatula or your hands and transfer to a flat surface dusted with flour and divide into two pieces.

Knead each piece lightly into a round with a rolling pin.

Roll them out to about a 20cm circle and then cut into 4.

Place on the griddle and bake for approx. 4 mins each side.

Allow to cool on a baking rack.

If you are going to make these a lot, get yourself a length of broom handle and use instead of a heavy rolling pin – old bakers tip!

Fruited white soda bread
– Robert Ditty

makes 1 loaf

300g self raising flour
pinch salt
30g sugar
2 tblsp olive oil
50g or more of washed dried fruit
200ml buttermilk

Sift the flour into a large bowl, add salt, sugar and sultanas and mix together. Make a well in the middle of the dry mixture. Mix the buttermilk and oil together and add to the dry ingredients.

Mix until all the dry ingredients are wet.

Transfer to a floured surface, then dust with flour and knead thoroughly into a round.

Place on a baking tray and press out to approx. 25cm diameter. Mark a cross shape into the dough with a knife.

Place in a heated oven of 210°C and bake for approx. 40 mins.

Sifting very important!

Potato bread
– Robert Ditty

makes 4 farls

227g mashed potato
63g plain white flour
12g melted butter or olive oil
pinch salt

Boil the potatoes, mash and allow to cool.

Sift the flour and salt, then add to potatoes with melted butter or olive oil.

Knead the mixture into a dough.

Divide into portions and pin out into required shapes.

Bake on a preheated griddle or a heavy pan.

Nick's wheaten bread

At the restaurant we add a small quantity of cracked wheat to give an extra nutty texture, however I don't think it is available in shops. If you can get it we add it at the rate of 400g/per kilo of flour and soak it in boiling water for half an hour before use. You may need less buttermilk if you go this route. We only started this after our supply of coarse flour from the watermill in Crossgar sadly ceased.

To source a good quality flour you may have to go to a health food store, as unfortunately we no longer have any old style water powered mills operating in Northern Ireland – unless you know different in which case we would love to hear from you!

makes 20 buns/2 small loaves

700g coarse stoneground wheaten flour
60g sugar /or honey
12g baking soda
12g cream of tartar
pinch salt
50g oil or melted butter
625ml buttermilk
sprinkle of seeds for the top

In a large bowl combine and mix all the dry ingredients.

Then add the oil and buttermilk and mix well so no pockets of dry flour are left, leaving quite a wet mix.

To make our wheaten buns we cook the mix in muffin tins at 180°C for about 20 mins. If cooking in a loaf tin it will take about 40 mins.

Sprinkle the poppy seeds, or any other that take your fancy, over the top before putting in the oven.

wheaten soda bread
– Robert Ditty

makes 4 loaves

400g wholemeal bread flour
40g course brown flour
150g soft plain flour
50g bakers bran or rolled oats
18g salt
18g bicarbonate of soda
50g local honey or sugar
50g melted butter or olive oil
1 lt buttermilk

Place all the dry ingredients into a suitable bowl and mix well by hand. Add the melted butter or olive oil and buttermilk until all the dry ingredients have been absorbed.

Deposit in suitable tins and dust each with bran or flour and mark a cross shape into the dough with a knife.

Place in a preheated oven at 230°C and bake for 20 mins, then reduce the heat to 200°C and bake for approx. a further 20 mins.

Corn bread

350g polenta
225g strong flour
3 tsp baking powder
85g caster sugar
4 eggs, beaten
600ml milk
1 x small tin sweetcorn

Mix all the dry ingredients thoroughly then add the beaten eggs and the milk, finally add the tin of sweetcorn and mix well. It is quite a wet mixture, a bit like a batter.

We usually cook the mix in a muffin tin so we get lots of little buns.

Cook at 170°C for about 30 mins or until well risen and golden brown.

Rye bread

makes 2 loaves

500g rye flour
500g strong white flour
100ml oil
1 dsp salt
30g fresh yeast
600ml lukewarm water
1 tblsp of caraway seeds [optional]

Sift the flours together in the mixing bowl of a mixer. Add the salt, the oil and half the caraway seeds, dissolving the yeast in the water.

Using the dough hook start mixing and add half the yeast and water mixture. Let it become incorporated and slowly add the rest of the liquid, don't let it become too wet. Knead the dough in the machine for about 5 mins longer if possible, then turn out and knead with your hands for 2–3 mins.

Then place in a floured bowl, cover with a damp cloth and put in a warm place to raise for about an hour. It should have doubled in size. Tip dough out onto a floured surface and knock all the air out of it, divide the dough in half with a knife and put into two loaf tins that you have coated with flour., Make a slash across the top of the dough with a sharp knife and put the loaves back in a warm place to do a second raise for about 30 mins.

If you like a shiny top glaze the loaves with egg yolk and milk beaten up together, just brush it on, sprinkle a few caraway seeds on top and bake at 200°C for approx 30 mins.

When cooked the bread should sound hollow when tapped on the bottom of the loaf. If cooked remove from the tin and allow to cool on a wire rack.

starters

Dips

We decided to offer a choice of dips on the menu at the Warehouse as a sort of recession beater as they are tasty and not expensive. We serve them in groups of 3 with either warmed pitta bread or vegetable crudités. Here is a selection for you to try.

Beetroot dip

Now, I don't really like beetroot, so you will be astonished to find 3 beetroot recipes in this book, and they would all convert an avid 'beetrootophobe' like me!

This recipe is pinched from Skye Gyngell's book *A year in my kitchen,* although I have amended her spice mix as some of the things she uses didn't appeal to me, and I was very happy with my version which we served at Granny Price's 90th birthday party.

1.5kg cooked beetroot
2 garlic cloves
1 large red chilli
bunch of coriander
½ bunch of mint leaves
3 tblsp balsamic vinegar
2 tblsp olive oil
125ml thick greek yoghurt
salt
1 tblsp grated horseradish or the best sauce you can get
pan roasted spice mix: 1 tblsp of coriander, cumin, fennel and mustard seeds ground in pestle and mortar

We like to scrub the whole beetroot.

Sprinkle a little salt and olive oil in with the whole beetroot and wrap it in foil. Bake in the oven for about 1 hour 30 mins at 175°C.

Put the beetroot, garlic and chilli in a food processor or blender, blitz and then add all the other ingredients.

Adjust the seasoning with salt and possibly add more balsamic.

Moroccan carrot dip

I am greatly taken with the flavours of the Moors and the Middle East, and this dip is evocative of these things. If you are ever in London try a wonderful restaurant called Moro – go for lunch and if you are a real foodie wander into Brindisa, a Spanish deli, a few doors down. Kathy tells me Sadlers Wells is just around the corner, so you can extend the experience to a great night too.

450g carrots
1 tsp harissa paste
3 cloves garlic
1 tsp ginger peeled and grated
1 tsp coriander seeds roasted and ground
1 tsp cumin roasted and ground
juice of 1 fresh lemon
2 tblsp olive oil

Cook the carrots until quite soft then blitz all the ingredients together until smooth in a food processor; might need a little sugar to balance the flavours.

Harissa is a fiery north African paste, which can be bought in tubes in a good deli and is a useful store cupboard ingredient – alternatively you can make it yourself – see page 113.

Hummous

A classic Middle Eastern dip, although, in Egypt, I believe they make it with dried broad beans where they are a great favourite. For Trevor's benefit this is heavily disguised chickpeas!

600g cooked chickpeas 3 cloves crushed garlic 200g tahini 1 green deseeded chilli, chopped 1 tblsp parsley 1 tblsp coriander, chopped 1 tblsp mint chopped 100ml olive oil salt and pepper	Soak the chickpeas overnight. Pour off the soaking water and put the chickpeas into a saucepan and cover with fresh water. Cook without salt until soft. Add the salt after cooking and save the cooking liquid – it is one of the best veggie stocks ever due to the high protein content in the chickpeas. Put the garlic, chilli and herbs into a food processor and blitz. Add the other ingredients and blitz again. If the mix is too dry add a little of the cooking liquid. Adjust the seasoning – it should have a slight kick from the chilli and a good flavour from the herbs. Serve with a little drizzle of olive oil on top.

Turkish almond dip

Really easy!

We sail in Turkey quite a lot and admire their food – it's a great melting pot with lots of different flavours. This dip is great if you are in a hurry and need to use store cupboard ingredients pronto!

125g white bread 35ml water 2 cloves garlic 200g ground almonds 25g toasted almonds 2 tblsp olive oil juice of 1 lemon	Soak the bread in the water and squeeze it out. Put lemon juice, bread, garlic, ground almonds and olive oil into a food processor and blitz. Slowly add water until soft consistency, sprinkle toasted almonds on top before serving.

Tapenade

This is not a true tapenade as it doesn't have capers in it, but it is very tasty and the sort of thing you can make very quickly from the store cupboard.

1 x 300g tin pitted green olives drained – I like the ones stuffed with white anchovies.
1 x 400g tin pitted black olives drained
3 cloves crushed garlic
290g jar sun dried tomatoes
1 dsp balsamic vinegar
4 anchovy fillets in oil
2 tblsp olive oil
salt and pepper to taste

Put all the ingredients into a food processor and blitz lightly to chop to a required texture. You may like it chunky or you may like it fine, it's up to you – just don't purée it too much.

Baba ganoush

It means 'my father is spoiled like a child by my mother'.

I think Jenny McCrea found this recipe way back in Kilmood days and it has been a favourite ever since.

3 aubergines
2 cloves garlic
½ jar tahini
juice of 1 lemon
2 tblsp Greek yoghurt
2 tblsp flat leaf parsley chopped
salt and pepper

Split the aubergines and coat with oil.

Grill till cooked through and soft. Some people remove the skin but I like the smoky flavour it gives the dish, and the colour is darker as well.

Blitz all the ingredients in a food processor and adjust seasoning to taste.

Big prawns with garlic saffron & chilli oil

I fell in love with these in a tapas bar in Northern Spain.

makes 2 portions

3 cloves garlic sliced
10 saffron strands soaked in boiling water
olive oil
½ tsp chilli flakes or 1 fresh deseeded chilli
200g prawns, as big as possible
You can use the cooked king prawns or economy version North Atlantic cooked prawns, or the luxury version, shelled langoustines, but make sure they are big ones.

Put the olive oil into a frying pan and heat gently to cook the garlic to a light golden colour.

Add the chilli flakes and the saffron strands plus water.

Finally add the prawns.

Heat through and serve with crusty bread.

Red pepper salsa

I have a thing about salsas and once you have mastered a basic one the sky is the limit. You can add all sorts of ingredients along with different herbs. The backbone for me is onions, garlic, tomatoes and vinegar/lemon juice and oil – oh – and a little chilli in some form is great too!

3 red peppers roasted and skinned
4 plum tomatoes, peeled
½ onion finely chopped
3 cloves garlic crushed
1 tblsp chopped fresh basil
1 chilli deseeded and chopped
2 tsp caster sugar
2 tblsp olive oil
juice of ½ lemon
salt and pepper

Dice the peppers into very small squares.

Cut tomatoes in half, take out all seeds and dice the flesh of the tomatoes to match the peppers.

Put the peppers and tomatoes into a bowl and add all the other ingredients.

Season to taste.

This is the base for all sorts of salsas and you can add any variety of other ingredients – go play!

Squid

Some people have a love hate relationship with squid, understandably as it can be like India rubber. The first secret is to get squid which is not too big – about 20cm long and try to get the fishmonger to clean it for you.

There are three ways to cook squid – very fast boiled/deep-fried or very slowly in a casserole. Although I have experimented with cooking large squid in a pressure cooker with various aromatics and it has worked quite well.

But… 'our squid' goes like this:

Fried spiced squid
on a thai cucumber salad with a soy chilli and ginger dressing

serves 6 people

800g squid
3 cups cornflour
2 tsp of chilli powder if you like it hot!
2 tblsp Chinese 5 spice powder
salt and pepper
oil for deep frying

If your fishmonger is willing get him to clean the squid. But don't buy big ones as they tend to be tough – about 15/16cm long in body is ideal and do keep the tentacles as they fry up beautifully for those who are not squeamish.

Once cleaned prepare squid as follows:

Slit up the inside of the tube – if not cleaned out remove all the guts and the thing that looks like a piece of plastic which is in fact its backbone. You now have a triangular piece of squid. Take a sharp heavy knife and cut in a criss-cross pattern very lightly just deep enough to pierce the flesh on the inside of the squid – this acts as a tenderising process. You end up with lots of lines like this…

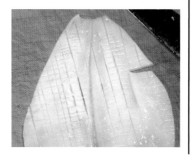

then cut into small pieces about 8cm square –
3 pieces should be enough for a starter portion.
When ready to deep fry coat in the cornflour mixed with 5 spice, chilli, salt and pepper and cook in very hot oil for about 3 mins until it turns a pale golden colour.

soy and chilli dressing

4 tblsp Ketjap Manis (Indonesian soy sauce)
100ml sesame oil
300ml sunflower oil
2 tblsp pickled ginger
1 tblsp hot chilli sauce or 1 large red chilli, deseeded and chopped
1 clove garlic crushed
1 tblsp fish sauce
toasted sesame seeds – add last

Mix all the ingredients except the toasted sesame seeds and blitz them in a liquidiser.

Add the sesame seeds.

Dress the cooked squid in a bowl or serve as a dipping sauce.

Cucumber salad

2 large cucumbers cut in half longways and
seeds scooped out then sliced
2 tblsp fresh coriander chopped
2 tblsp fresh mint chopped
1 red chilli deseeded and finely chopped
juice of 1 lemon
soft brown sugar to taste
2 tblsp toasted sesame seeds

Mix all the salad ingredients in a bowl and set aside until needed.

Place the cucumber salad on plates and set the squid pieces on top, pour over the soy and chilli dressing, garnish with fresh coriander.

Moules marinières

butter
½ onion, finely chopped
3 cloves of garlic, crushed
1 heaped tblsp chopped parsley
1kg mussels – you will need to rinse these and de-beard them. Feel along the front of the shells and you will find a little fibrous membrane, pull this out. Discard any mussels that are lying open. Just tap them to see if they close first.
250ml dry white wine

In a large saucepan with a lid melt the butter and fry the onion and garlic.

Now add the parsley and the mussels, finally add the white wine.

Put the lid on and cook for about five minutes or until the shells are well opened.

You can eat these as they are or you can remove the meats and put into another dish.

The stock or juice can be strained through a muslin cloth or a clean tea towel and I like to use it to make my beurre blanc – see page 78.

31

Gravadlax

Prep time 3 days – but only 10 mins assembly

The name means 'buried salmon', literally. Sadly the wild salmon is hard to come by these days but when we first started making this dish it was in June or July when we got the first run of wild fish. This recipe is for a whole fish that has been filleted – if you just want 1 fillet divide this recipe in half.

One fillet will do starters for about 12 portions, but it keeps well and is a great snack to have in the fridge.

1 whole salmon filleted and pin bones removed – about 4kg or 2kg per side
dill, chopped, 2 packets 50g each
100g soft brown sugar
100g salt
80g crushed black pepper i.e., crushed quite coarsely with a pestle and mortar

In a shallow roasting tray (i.e., one with a lip about 10cm deep) lay the two fillets of salmon side by side.

Cover both with the salt and sugar mixed together with the crushed pepper and finally with the dill.

Now lay the fillets face to face, or dill to dill, and cover with cling film. Put a tray with a weight on top into the fridge and leave for 3 days. Each day you turn the fish over. If you do just one fillet, cut in half and put one piece on top of the other.

Open it up and baste it with the lovely juices in the tray then reassemble and weight again.

To serve, slice very thinly like smoked salmon and lay on a plate, make a mustard and dill vinaigrette and serve with wheaten bread. You can either slice it like smoked salmon or we just cut it vertically and it looks more Scandinavian somehow!

Mustard and dill vinaigrette

30g English mustard
10g caster sugar
40g white wine vinegar
170g oil (sunflower is good)
2 tblsp chopped dill
1 tblsp yellow mustard seeds

Put mustard, sugar and vinegar into a jar.

Put the lid on and shake vigorously.

Now add half of the oil and shake again.

Repeat with the remainder of the oil and then add the dill. The dressing should be thick.

Celeriac remoulade

A wonderfully useful vegetable, but I have never had much success growing them in Ireland. We use celeriac in soups to give a creamy texture without the cream, but we also make this classic French bistro dish. It comes in various forms – see additions below the main recipe.

serves 6

800g celeriac
200ml mayonnaise
6 drops Tabasco
1 tblsp capers
1 tblsp English mustard

Peel the celeriac and cut into julienne or matchsticks which is best done with a mandolin cutter but watch your fingers!

If you don't have a mandolin just coarsely grate the celeriac, however the texture won't be as good.

Now fold in the mayonnaise, the mustard and the Tabasco. Like all mayonnaise salads you want it moist but not sloppy with dressing.

Now add the capers and any of the other ingredients that you wish. Season with salt and pepper.

Other possible additions are horseradish and or fresh white crab meat. A chef friend serves the horseradish version with smoked salmon and I think it works very well

Thai style vegetables with peanut dressing

The Thai people are not only lovely in manner and looks: they make great food with amazing flavours. My first encounter was in one of London's first Thai restaurants many years ago and we had this salad. It took me a while to imitate it, but I think this works well.

pickle

1 lt of white wine vinegar
1 lt of water
4 cups of white sugar
2 cloves of garlic, crushed
3cm knob of ginger, chopped
salt

Put all the ingredients into a saucepan and bring to the boil.

Allow to cool. Once cool, add the prepared vegetables and marinade for 4–6 hours.

vegetables

cabbage
carrot
mangetout
celery
peppers
ginger
Plus anything else that grabs your fancy!

Cut and slice all vegetables finely and prettily, making enough to be covered by the pickle mix above.

sauce

one 227g jar crunchy peanut butter
2 cloves garlic
3cm ginger
a little chilli in any form (to taste)
some of the vinegar marinade from the pickle

Whiz up the garlic, chilli and ginger in a food processor. Add the peanut butter and the marinade vinegar to achieve desired consistency, i.e. quite thick.

Drain the vegetables, saving the marinade for future use and dress the vegetables with sauce as required.

Sprinkle with toasted sesame seeds if you like them.

pâtés

I have always enjoyed making pâtés of different kinds and marvelled on visits to France, when I lived there as a young man, at the diversity in the local traiteurs or charcuteries and enjoyed many an alfresco lunch of crusty bread and pâté. In France people are proud of the fact that they have sourced a product from a specialist purveyor and would say so at the dinner table, not always the case at home I suspect.

Terrine
a basic recipe – for variations see below

This recipe makes 2 loaf tins – 16 generous portions

equipment

Mincer; loaf tin; foil; baking parchment; large weight – if you don't have a mincer but do have a good relationship with your butcher you might persuade him to mince all the ingredients for you. However, when we did it a few times our butcher got a few complaints from a little old lady who said that one time, when I gave him a mix to make sausages, that his own brand came out spicy and garlicky! The moral of the tale is do it last thing in the day .

3 medium onions, peeled and sliced
3 cloves garlic, crushed
1 tblsp each of thyme, parsley, rosemary, chopped
butter
650g pork belly
650g streaky bacon
450g chicken livers (hold some back for layering) make sure to remove the bile ducts!

4 tblsp port
4 tblsp brandy
1 good dsp of salt, a good grind of black pepper
1 dsp yellow mustard seeds
1 dsp coriander seeds
2 dsp green peppercorns in brine – rinsed
50g back bacon to line the tins

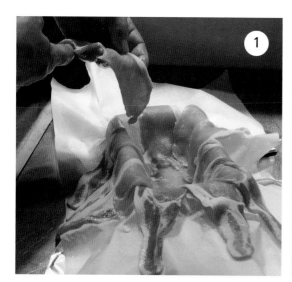

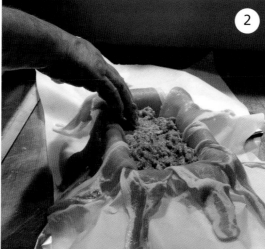

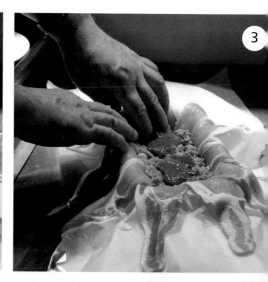

Melt the butter, add the onions, garlic and herbs, cook for 10 mins on a low heat and allow to cool a little.

In a large bowl mix up the meats and the onion mixture. Mince all together with quite a coarse mincing plate (I use 10mm).

When all the ingredients are minced, add the seasonings to the terrine mixture, i.e. seeds, peppercorns, salt, pepper, port and brandy. It will need quite a lot of seasoning as the fat content seems to use up all the flavour somehow. To check the seasoning, make a little patty and fry in a pan. Once you are happy with the flavour it is time to assemble the terrine for cooking.

Take a loaf tin and line it, first with foil and then baking parchment, leaving enough spare at the edges to completely wrap up the terrine.

1 Line the tin with back bacon so that the bacon is long enough to encase the terrine when the tin is full.

2 Now fill the tin half full with the terrine mixture.

3 Take the livers you have reserved and lay a line of them down the middle of the tin then cover with more terrine mixture.

4 Make sure the top of the terrine is slightly domed like a loaf of bread. This is to assist with pressing after it's cooked.

5 Wrap the bacon over the top so that you cannot see any terrine mixture then fold over the parchment and foil.

Now put the terrine in a deep roasting tray and put water in the tray to about half way up the depth of the terrine.

Put into an oven at 150° and cook for 1½ hours. If you possess a temperature probe aim for 73°.

Remove from the oven, drain the water off the pan, put a tray and a heavy weight on top immediately and refrigerate.

This last bit is most important as it makes the terrine bond together and makes it easy to cut an attractive slice. Chill overnight.

Cut a slice off the loaf and serve with toast and a homemade chutney (see pages 116–7).

Don't be tempted to slice it up before you are ready to serve it, as the meat will oxidise and look rather grey and unappetising.

variations

Once you have mastered the basic mix you can add different meats like venison, or duck. You can also layer some cuts of these meats along with the livers or if you are feeling very extravagant you could use some foie gras. Some may like to also add pistachios as they give a nice green colour but be aware of the dreaded nut allergies.

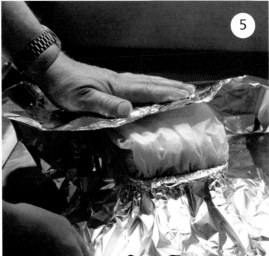

Chicken liver parfait

A big favourite that finds its way onto the menu especially around Christmas time
as it is quick and easy to make.

And very tasty!

450g chicken livers
2 tblsp port
1 tblsp brandy
salt
1 clove garlic, crushed
white pepper
225g butter

Melt the butter and allow to cool a little. Pick through the livers to remove any sinew and the bile duct (dark green pouch full of bitter liquid), and any discoloured meat around the duct.

Blitz the livers, port, brandy and garlic in a liquidiser and then pass through a fine strainer. Now add the melted butter and blitz again. Seasoning is very central so cook some in a pan to check.

Line a loaf tin with foil, then with clingfilm, leaving enough spare to envelop the parfait mixture once you pour it in.

Parcel it up with the foil so it is sealed all around and cook in a bain marie (water bath) at 110° for about 1 hour 15 mins. Chill overnight and serve with toast or melba toast and chutney.

If you want to make it look classy whip up some butter until very soft, trim the parfait to a nice regular flat shape and with a palette knife thinly spread each surface with butter. Do three sides, allow to sit in the fridge and then do the final side. Try to keep an even depth of butter if possible.

Chicken liver pâté à la Kathy

Kathy doesn't cook very often now the boys are long gone but then why have a dog and bark yourself! This is a recipe she found years ago and it's great – tasty and easy to make. Somehow, when I make it it's not as good as hers. My sister Sue uses a healthier variation of this recipe with less butter.

500g chicken livers
4 cloves garlic, crushed
2 medium onions, peeled and chopped
4–6 tsp thyme – fresh, just the leaves
250g butter
2 tblsp brandy
salt and pepper

Pick over the chicken livers to remove any sinew or nasty green bits from the bile duct.

In half of the butter fry the onions, garlic and herbs to soften and caramelise, then put into food processor.

Now cook the chicken livers very lightly in the rest of the butter until just set but still quite pink.

Add the brandy and flame it to remove the alcohol then remove it from the heat.

Put the chicken livers into the food processor with onions etc., and blitz until smooth. Check the seasoning and flavour to taste. Pour the mixture into a bowl or individual ramekins to set in the fridge.

The pâté can be sealed with more melted butter on top but frankly your heart could do without it.

Serve with toast and chutney or crusty bread for a light lunch.

Tarts – because real men don't eat quiche!

When I lived in France with the Mathieu family, Madame was an amazing cook. She hailed from Alsace the home of – you've guessed it – quiche lorraine!

Help! I seem to be stuck in a French charcuterie time warp but we have always had a tart on the menu at Nick's. Maybe we should call it Quiche as it's a lot easier than going up to a table and asking who is the tart! Normally it contains fish and it is one of the first things the young chefs get to make after they have mastered soup making.

In fact, there are a few regular customers who never order anything else.

pastry

23cm flan dish
Any kind of fish such as smoked haddock, salmon, crab
60g butter + 60g cookeen
250g flour
1 egg
cold water
pinch salt

We cook the fish first as it doesn't cook as well in the custard.

When lining a flan case with pastry always leave a good lip or flap around the outside edge to allow for shrinkage and you can trim it off once cooked.

Cook the flan case 'blind' in a low oven at about 150°C. The idea is to get a base cooked through but without colour. When taken out of the oven brush the inside of the pastry case with eggwash (an egg beaten with a little milk). This makes a waterproof layer and stops the pastry going soggy. Put it back into the oven for 5 mins to seal it.

filling – custard

2 eggs, 1 yolk
200ml whipping/single cream
salt and pepper
60g grated mature cheddar or other cheese of choice
2 small leeks, washed sliced and fried in butter to soften
approx. 200g of fish per flan case

Now layer up the tart with the fish, some herbs and the cheese. Pour in the savoury custard making sure the fish is completely submerged. Bake in the oven at 180°C for about 30 mins or until the custard is set and you have a nice golden brown colour to the tart.

Variations are as broad as your imagination, but the ones we find work well are:

Onion – fried to caramelise with gruyère or Glebe Brethren cheese and savoury custard
Mixed seafood, i.e. cooked mussels, prawns bits of various fish
Asparagus
Goat's cheese is good with the onion mixture
Classic bacon & cheese (quiche lorraine)

starters

40

soups

I have always said that if a cook can make a good soup then there's a fair chance we can make them a good chef.

Turkey broth à la grand-mère

Christmas in the Price household is always a time of complete exhaustion as you can imagine, but it is always a collective effort with so many good cooks in the house. In spite of all the 'grande bouffe' of the day itself, the thing my boys Adam and Ben looked forward to most was the massive pot of turkey broth that I usually made on boxing day. It used to sustain them and their friends on return from the pub over the festive season followed, of course, by their mum's trifle!

This will make a big pot of broth – enough for maybe 30 portions

ingredients for stock

You can of course use a chicken but for me the turkey just has the edge on flavour
1 roast turkey carcass
2 onions chopped
6 sticks of celery peeled and chopped
3 carrots peeled and chopped
2 bay leaves
water to cover the other ingredients by about 10cm

Boil all of the ingredients for about an hour in a large saucepan, strain and reserve the carcass and the stock.

Pick any meat off the bones and put aside.

ingredients for broth

3 onions sliced
4 carrots peeled and grated or cut into matchsticks on a mandolin
1 head of celery washed and coarse outer stalks peeled. All chopped, including the leaves
3 cloves of garlic peeled and sliced
long grain rice – 4 tblsp
6 leeks split longways, washed and sliced
butter or oil to cook
chopped parsley to garnish

Heat oil or butter in a big saucepan.

Seal off the onions and garlic then add the leeks, celery and carrots.

Cook slowly for 7–8 mins. Now add the reserved stock and the rice. Simmer for about 20 mins. Put the turkey meat back in and check for flavour and seasoning. If you haven't got enough meaty flavour out of your stock you can add a little piece of stock cube.

Serve in a bowl with a good sprinkle of chopped parsley.

Minestrone

Ok it's lots of chopping but it is worth it. Possibly more of an Ulster slant on an Italian classic but well worth the effort. It's almost a meal in a bowl.

serves 10

oil

100g bacon chopped (if using instead of ham hock, if veggie ignore)

2 onions sliced

3 cloves garlic crushed

2 potatoes cubed

½ cauliflower in florets

¼ drumhead or hard cabbage sliced

2 tblsp tomato purée

2 courgettes sliced into sticks

2 carrots sliced

I tblsp chopped fresh basil

2 x 400g tin of chopped tomatoes

3 celery sticks peeled to remove stringy bits and cut into batons

1 tin of white beans, cannellini are good

basil and parmesan to garnish

2 lt chicken or vegetable stock depending on your preference. If you want to be a real star you have to boil a ham hock and make a stock that way, i.e. using the liquid you have cooked the hock in.

I add some ingredients after I have made the soup as they deteriorate in colour and texture if cooked in the soup –
green beans trimmed and lightly cooked
peas, fresh ideally, but frozen are fine
cooked pasta like farfalle or some other small attractive shape.

Put the oil into a deep saucepan and warm up over a moderate heat.

Cook bacon, if using, then add onions and garlic until softened.

Next add the cabbage, cauliflower, celery, carrots and potatoes. Cook for 5 mins and then add the tomato purée. Cook for 2–3 mins.

Now add the tomatoes, the beans and stock. If you have a cooked ham hock it goes in now. Simmer for about 20–25 mins or until the potatoes are cooked. Taste and adjust the seasoning.

Remove the ham hock and shred the meat, put it back into the pot to serve.

Add the peas, green beans and cooked pasta. Warm them through.

Put a portion into a deep bowl and sprinkle with chopped basil.

Serve with a side of grated parmesan.

Just don't expect your guests to eat anything else.

Chowder

It is all about flavour and one of the best I ever tasted was in a little pub in Roundstone called McDowds, I think. A big bowl of chowder, a pint of stout, and then a long walk along the strand. All whilst riding a bike around the 'circuit' from Clifden to Maam Cross in the rain – oh what a holiday! I came back inspired to make my own. It can be a starter or even a meal in a bowl on its own.

serves 8

Ingredients	Method
400g smoked haddock 120g onions 130g smoked bacon 3 cloves garlic crushed 2 green peppers sliced 340g tin sweetcorn 750g potatoes, peeled and cubed into 10 mm dices 300g leeks, washed and sliced 1 lt milk butter/oil 1 lt fish stock, if stuck you can use chicken stock	Poach the haddock in the milk, drain and reserve the milk and fish separately. Melt the butter and sweat off the onions, peppers, garlic and leeks then add the potatoes and sweetcorn. Cook for 4 mins, then add the fish stock and cook for about 20 mins or until the potatoes are cooked. When soft, add the milk and half the fish. Drain the liquid off and divide the solids into two halves liquidising half the solids with all the liquid to give a thick chunky soup. Now return the remaining fish, adjust the seasoning and to serve add a little cream and a little chopped herbs – chives or parsley.

Lentil soup

Lentils red, lentils green, lentils brown and lentils puy are all just great and so versatile for all manner of soups and veggie dishes from loaf to fritter. High in protein and fibre, I just love 'em.

serves 8

Ingredients	Method
250g red lentils, rinsed 250g onion, sliced 2 cloves garlic peeled and crushed 1 courgette washed and chopped 1 carrot peeled and chopped 225g leeks washed and chopped 125g celery peeled and chopped 2.5 lt chicken or veggie stock – ham stock is brilliant also butter or oil to sweat veg	Sweat off the onion and garlic to soften, then add all the other vegetables and cook for about 5 mins on a gentle heat. Now add the lentils and cook for a further 3 mins, next pour in the stock and simmer gently until the carrots and lentils are cooked through. Purée the soup and correct the seasoning. **variations** Add chilli, cumin and tomato – works great!

Leek and potato soup

This recipe is a great favourite of mine. It can also be served chilled and with the addition of cream you can call it Vichychoisse, but in fact it is good old leek and potato.

I made it once in Washington DC in a very smart restaurant and the head chef said it was too salty. I couldn't possibly print what I thought and after all it was his restaurant. The secret of this soup is lots of leeks to give good colour and flavour.

serves 10

850g stewing leeks
2 onions [350g]
3 garlic cloves
1kg potatoes peeled
3 lt chicken stock
butter or oil for frying

Cut the leeks lengthwise and wash grit out of the leaves under the tap, then slice in half moon shapes. Use some of the dark green bits for colour but be aware that they can be a bit fibrous and stringy.

Peel and slice the onions and squash the garlic, cube the potatoes into 2–3cm dices.

Melt some butter or oil in a deep saucepan, add the onions and garlic and sweat briefly to soften over a gentle heat. Next add the leeks and cook for a further 4 mins, add the potato and cook for a further 5 mins.

Now add the stock and cook for about 20 mins until the potato is soft. Remove from heat and liquidise.

Taste, adjust the seasoning and when serving add a little cream and garnish with a few chopped chives.

Mushroom soup

or to be classically correct mushroom velouté

This is one of the few soups that we make that contains flour. Basically you make a roux with mushrooms and vegetables in it and add stock. The most important part of any roux-based soup or sauce is to cook out the butter and flour mixture to get rid of the floury taste and to stop the bottom of the pot sticking!

200g onion [1 medium] peeled and chopped
500g mushrooms sliced – save about 100g for garnish
I carrot [150g] peeled and chopped
2 sticks of celery peeled and chopped
50g flour
25g butter
1 lt chicken or vegetable stock

serves 6

Melt the butter and sweat off the onions, then add the leeks carrot and celery and cook for a few mins.

Add the mushrooms and cook a little more, turn the heat down and mix the flour in cooking it out gently for 7–8 mins.

Gradually add the stock and cook the soup gently until the carrots are cooked, about 20 or 25 mins.

Then purée and adjust the seasoning to serve.

Fry off the remaining sliced mushrooms in butter and put some into each bowl topping off with a little cream and some chopped chives or parsley.

variations

Put in a few dried, soaked porcini or other wild mushrooms to intensify flavour but be sure you know what they are!

Chestnut and porcini soup

We ate this soup served in little shot glasses in a wonderful Gascon 'tapas' bar in London. It was extremely rich but awfully good, so when I came home I had a go at recreating it.

serves 4

butter
2 onions peeled and sliced
3 cloves garlic, crushed
200g large breakfast mushrooms, sliced, the chestnut ones are good
30g porcini/cepe, fresh is great but dried and soaked in boiling water for 20 mins is fine
3 carrots, peeled and chopped
2 leeks, washed and sliced
4 stalks celery
250g frozen chestnuts – or a 240g tin or indeed dried and reconstituted from a health food shop
1.5 lt chicken stock
cream
truffle oil [optional]

Melt the butter in a large pan then add the onions and garlic and sweat to soften. Add the leeks, celery and carrots. Cook for 5 mins and then add the sliced mushrooms and cook for a couple of minutes.

Now add the chestnuts and the dried porcini plus the soaking water – watch the bottom of the water as it is often a bit gritty.

Finally add the stock and cook until the carrots and chestnuts are soft, then purée, season and serve with a little cream and a dash of truffle oil if you are feeling extravagant!

Beetroot soup

As far as I am concerned this is Jenny's soup.

I never really believed that this is all that went into it but it is true and delicious, and the colour is awesome!

serves 4–5

3 large onions
8 beetroot (1.2kg) peeled and cut into cubes
½ small lemon, cut into quarters
2 lt stock, chicken or vegetable

garnish
horseradish and sour cream

Put all the ingredients into a large pan and bring to the boil.

Cook until well softened – about 30 mins and then remove the lemons and strain through a sieve.

Serve with a dollop of sour cream mixed with good horseradish or even better grated root of horseradish.

One of our managers was courting strong with a lovely lady who later became his wife. He always finished telephone conversations to her by saying, 'see you, love you', which is lovely, except that one day, he was taking a table reservation off a customer and for some reason signed off in the same manner, much to the customer's amusement!

Carrot soup with ginger & coriander spice

When our boys were small, Kathy made two soups. Orange soup and green soup depending on the contents of the fridge, or pantry, on the day. The orange one quite often contained carrot or sometimes swede/turnip, the green one leeks and green lentils – this is an orange one!

serves 6

butter/oil
1 large (200g) onion, peeled and sliced
1kg carrots, peeled and chopped
1 medium leek, split washed and sliced
2 sticks celery peeled and chopped
40g root ginger peeled and chopped
1 dsp coriander seeds (roasted in a frying pan and ground in a pestle & mortar)
[or cheat and use ground but it's not so good].
2.25 lt stock, chicken or vegetable

Melt the butter/oil in a saucepan and sweat off the vegetables.

Add the ginger, the coriander and the stock.

Cook until the carrots are cooked through, purée and adjust the seasoning.

variation

Add Thai green curry paste and coconut milk for 'Thai carrot soup'.

Dutch pea soup

A classic thick pea soup which I first made many years ago for a Dutch Week promotion in Manchester.

serves 6

onions peeled and sliced
3 cloves garlic, peeled and crushed
300g frozen peas
250g split green peas soaked overnight and drained
130g carrots, peeled and chopped
200g leeks split, washed and sliced
350g celeriac peeled and cubed
ham for garnish in strips
butter/oil
stock – chicken, ham or vegetable

Heat the oil and butter in a saucepan; add onions, garlic, carrot, leeks and celeriac. Sweat off gently for 5 mins. Now add the split peas and the stock and cook for about half-an-hour until the peas and carrots are soft.

Now add the frozen peas which will give a great colour boost and a lovely fresh taste, then purée the soup.

Adjust the seasoning to taste.

The Dutch eat this as a very thick soup – I prefer it a little wetter.

On serving put some slices of ham in each bowl – good ham mind you, none of your plastic slices!

French onion soup

One of the first 'French' dishes I ever cooked. Some think it's too rich, too oniony, too sweet, too salty, and yes, it may well be all of these but with a big gruyère topped croûton what could make you feel better on a cold winters day? Plus it's very quick to make!

serves 6

30g butter and 1 tblsp oil
1kg onions peeled and sliced along the lines
handful of fresh thyme
6 small sprigs rosemary
4 cloves garlic peeled crushed
750ml chicken or beef stock
100g gruyère cheese grated
French bread for croûtons

Heat the oil and butter in a pan. Add onions, garlic, thyme and rosemary. Cook until they are well caramelised and brown without burning. You can achieve this by adding a tiny bit of stock every now and again to stop it burning.

Add the rest of the stock and simmer for about 20 mins.

It should be like a thick onion stew.

To serve make French bread croûtons by toasting thick slices of the bread and top with grated gruyère cheese.

Fill bowls with soup, croûtons on top, and put bowls and all under the grill to melt the cheese!

Gazpacho

This is the most refreshing soup on a hot day which I first encountered in the mountains inland from Nerja in Southern Spain. I just couldn't get enough and had to learn how to make it myself. Different areas have variations on the recipe.

serves 4–5

1 medium red onion
1 tsp garlic crushed
1kg tomatoes – peeled
1 cucumber
3 red peppers
2 tblsp wine vinegar
150ml olive oil
110g white bread – crusts removed
200ml water
salt and pepper

In a bowl, soak the bread in the water, then squeeze the water out again with your hands.

Put onion, garlic tomatoes, cucumber, red peppers, soaked bread in a liquidiser with a little water to make it blitz properly. Blitz for 1 minute and then add the wine vinegar and the olive oil.

Season to taste. If too thick add more water or ice cubes if you are in a hurry as I always am! Chill for 3 hours if you can.

As our tomatoes are never ripe the soup may need sugar.

Garnish with garlic croûtons and finely chopped bits of the vegetables in the recipe. Some Spanish people also add ground almonds but these are optional.

The end result should be quite wet and garlicky.

Mediterranean seafood soup

I can't remember the first time we made this soup – just that it always takes a lot of fixing at the end, and it is quite labour intensive to make. But like all things in cooking it rewards the effort, and it's quite possible you may break your food processor!

serves 6

1 onion sliced
2 leeks washed and chopped
3 cloves of garlic crushed
1 chilli deseeded and chopped
2 heads fennel peeled and chopped
saffron (6 strands cooked in boiling water)
2 oranges zest and juice
1 dsp Pernod
8 large prawn heads or shells
400g tinned tomatoes
1 tblsp tomato purée
2 fish heads [I used a couple of sea bream heads the last time.]
1.5 lt water
olive oil

Heat the olive oil and fry the onions, garlic, prawns, fish heads, fennel, leeks, chilli flakes, saffron and orange zest for 5–6 mins.

Add the tomato purée and cook for another 3–4 mins. Then add the water, fish heads and tinned tomatoes.

Simmer for 20 mins, then purée the whole lot.

I suggest you put the dry matter with very little liquid through a robust food processor.

It maybe a good idea to smash up the shells with a rolling pin first. The last time I made it for the book, it went all over the place! Finally pass through a fine sieve.

Taste and correct.

Next – 'the Fixing'! You need to use your fixing palette of chilli, pernod, saffron, orange/lemon juice, salt, pepper, sugar.

It has to end up rich and full flavoured. Serve with a big rouille topped croûton – see page 111 for rouille recipe.

meat and poultry

Ok, either you like meat or you don't.
That's fine, but if you do, I feel that it's important that the beast has the best life it can before feeding us. So, it follows, please buy the best quality that you can afford because, for example, to taste a piece of rare breed pork against industrially reared pork, will be a revelation.

A lot of people don't like offal, based on memories of school dinners, where liver was something powdery and dry. Oh, the food scars! But then in my teenage years a revelation – I was introduced to calf's liver in France, and later devilled kidneys, and oh, the sheer joy of foie gras with px sherry…
When cooked properly, our customers love offal too, and when on the menu at the Warehouse, it flies out.

Liver with onion gravy

the gravy

serves 4

2 onions peeled and sliced (300g)
2 cloves garlic crushed
1 dsp tomato purée
500ml chicken stock
2 sprigs of fresh rosemary and thyme
(dried if not available fresh)
butter and oil
couple of drops of gravy browning
cornflour if required

Heat the oil/butter in a saucepan.

Add the onions, garlic and herbs. Sweat down until they are nicely caramelised – going brown, and now add the tomato purée.

Cook a little and then add the chicken stock and a couple of drops of gravy browning. Cook for about 30 mins.

Thicken if required with a little cornflour and water.

the liver

liver (either calf's or lamb's 160g /per person)
flour seasoned with salt and pepper sufficient to coat liver

We always cut from a whole liver and are always careful to trim off the outside skin as it can be very chewy. So first, check the top rim of your slice of liver and if it is shiny just trim it off with a sharp knife.

Heat oil/butter in a frying pan. Toss the liver in seasoned flour and gently fry.

Ideally, you want to serve it pink so don't overcook it or it will be like my school memories!

Serve with some buttery mashed potato and the onion gravy, Aahh! Comfort food.

The gravy is great with sausages too.

Braised ox cheek

Whilst looking for items for our set menu Jilly Dougan, one of our more knowledgable suppliers, offered us beef or ox cheeks, a great piece of meaty well exercised muscle which when cooked slowly takes on a wonderful unctuous quality. Great comfort food, although, it was referred to as, 'a slightly uncouth big lump of meat', but we have developed a sexier presentation – though it's still great on buttery mash!

This also cooks very well in a slow cooker taking about 8 hours on medium.

serves 4–5 people

4 ox cheeks
1 onion sliced
3 cloves garlic crushed
3 sticks celery peeled and cut into matchsticks
2 carrots
5 mushrooms sliced
oil
1 tblsp tomato purée
500ml good dark ale like Clotworthy Dobbin from Kilkeel
1 lt beef stock

Trim the meat and take off any sinew or silverskin.

Heat the oil in a deep, thick bottomed pan. Seal the beef and get a little colour and caramelise the meat. Then lift out the meat.

Fry the onion and garlic to soften. Add the mushrooms and cook for 2–3 mins then add the celery, carrots and tomato purée.

Mix well, cook for 3 or 4 mins, then add the beer making sure to loosen all the beef sediment in the pan.

Bring to the boil and cook off the alcohol.

Add the beef stock making sure the meat is well covered with liquid. Bring back to the boil and cover with a lid. Cook at about 160ºC for 2 hours. At this stage you may want to thicken the sauce and adjust the seasoning.

The meat is sliceable and is great served with some buttery mashed potato topped with the rich gravy.

meat

Devilled kidneys

People say they don't like the strong taste of kidneys, but we have a solution.

Peel the thin membrane off the outside of the kidney then slice in half long-ways, remove the fatty sinew in the middle and soak in milk for about 4 hours.

serves 2 as a main course or 4 as a starter

8 lamb kidneys, skinned, trimmed and cut in half
1 tblsp plain flour
salt
cayenne pepper
2 tblsp good made up English mustard
Worcestershire sauce
150ml chicken stock
50g butter
chopped parsley
4 slices of good quality white crusty bread, toasted and buttered

Toss the kidneys in the flour mixed with some salt and cayenne pepper.

Melt the butter in a frying pan and cook the kidneys for about 5 mins. They should be pink inside. Now add the mustard, Worcestershire sauce and chicken stock.

Simmer to thicken the sauce and serve at once on the hot buttered toast, with a good four grinds of black pepper and lots of chopped parsley.

Lamb shanks

These are another big favourite at the Warehouse. We always use the shanks from the rear legs as we find the front shanks a bit small.

The method is similar to the cheeks but we tend to use red wine and rosemary in the liquor.

serves 4

4 lamb shanks (rear leg)
1 onion, peeled and sliced
3 cloves crushed garlic
2 carrots, peeled and chopped
2 sticks of celery, peeled and chopped
3 bay leaves
2 sprigs rosemary
375ml red wine
1 tblsp tomato purée
olive oil
1 lt lamb stock (or beef)

Seal off the lamb shanks in a saucepan with some oil, to colour, then lift out. Sweat off the onions, garlic and herbs in the same pan.

Add the carrot, celery and tomato purée, mix in well and cook for a couple of mins. Add the red wine, boil for about 3–4 mins then add the stock and bring back to a simmer. Cover and cook in the oven at 140°C for about 2½ hours until lamb is tender.

Check seasoning and thicken sauce if required.

Lamb chops with rosemary scented red wine lentils

I adore lamb chops. I know lots of chefs like to serve racks and lollipops and canons and all the other sexy cuts but I just enjoy the flavour and the crispy fat and being able to pick up the bone and chew it, to which end Kathy always insists we serve a fingerbowl, when they are on the menu.

serves 4

8 lamb chops
2 onions, sliced
2 cloves garlic, crushed
rosemary
2 tblsp tomato purée
75cl red wine
1 lt lamb stock
olive oil to fry
300g puy lentils or large green ones if puy are not available

Sweat off onion, garlic and rosemary in olive oil in a saucepan until the onions are transparent. Add the tomato purée and cook for 2 mins.

Add red wine and simmer for 10 mins to get rid of the alcohol. Add lamb stock and reduce for 30 mins.

Meanwhile wash the lentils and cook lightly in lamb stock with a few sprigs of rosemary and some salt to the desired consistency, which is until they are soft, but have a little bite in them. Drain and reserve.

Strain the red wine sauce through a sieve and mix with the lentils. Season to personal taste.

The lamb chops are usually grilled and placed on a bed of the sauce, it looks great in a large white bowl style of plate.

Simply garnish with fresh rosemary.

Fragrant lamb

This dish was inspired by the slow braises of Chinese cookery, but here I have used Thai flavours, and it works really well. I have used it for large numbers at a party and as long as you don't overcook it, it keeps warm well and looks great on the plate with plain boiled rice.

serves 6

1 leg of lamb, cubed
2 small onions sliced
3 large assorted colour peppers
3 cloves of garlic, crushed
2 lime leaves
50g coriander chopped
vegetable oil to fry
1 tblsp green Thai curry paste
2 tblsp tomato purée
1 tin coconut milk
lamb or chicken stock to cover
½ jar pickled ginger
Ketjap Manis soy sauce to taste
brown sugar to taste
cornflour and water to thicken

Fry off the lamb in small batches to seal and remove from the pan.

Fry the onions, peppers, garlic and lime leaves in the same pan you used for the meat. Add the curry paste and tomato purée and cook for 5 mins. Return the meat and stir well, then add the coconut milk and stock to cover the meat.

Now add the chopped coriander, the pickled ginger, Ketjap Manis and sugar to taste. Cook until the meat is just tender. It is best cooked the day before and allowed to stand overnight to develop all the flavours.

To serve reheat, ensuring it is heated well through, and then thicken as required. Serve with rice or noodles and maybe a spicy Thai carrot salad.

Lasagne

Because Simon McCance, now chef patron of Ginger, part of the Nick's Warehouse diaspora says I have to put it in here. The funny thing being that we only ever served it for staff wine tastings and training sessions, but it must have hit a chord!

Bolognese | **serves 6**

2 onions chopped
2 bay leaves
3 garlic, crushed
2 carrots grated
4 sticks of celery peeled and chopped
500g lean mince
800g chopped tinned tomatoes
1 tblsp tomato purée
1 lt beef stock
375ml red wine
lots of fresh parsley, basil, oregano and
3 bay leaves
oil

Sweat off the onions and garlic in the oil. Add the grated carrot and chopped celery. Now add the minced beef and brown evenly. Add the purée mixing well and then the tomatoes, stock and red wine. This has to simmer for about 1½ hours.

To finish add all the herbs and adjust the flavour with tomato ketchup and a little Worcestershire sauce. It should be quite wet – if not add more stock or, if well flavoured, a little water.

The meat sauce has to be quite wet as it helps cook the raw pasta.

cheese sauce

50g butter
50g flour
400ml hot milk
200g grated mature cheddar
pinch cayenne
salt and pepper
lasagne sheets

Melt the butter and add the flour. Cook gently for about 5 mins to a sandy texture. It is important to avoid a floury flavour in the sauce. Now slowly add the milk and beat it in to avoid lumps. When all the milk is incorporated add the cheese and mix it in well.

Season with a pinch of cayenne, salt and pepper.

In a rectangular ovenproof dish, coat the bottom with the cheese sauce, add a layer of pasta then a layer of meat. Repeat this process – sauce, another layer of pasta, meat, sauce, pasta, cheese sauce, pasta, meat, sauce, pasta and finally top with a layer of cheese sauce.

Bake at 170°C for 40 mins and serve with a nice crunchy salad.

Meatloaf

Some dishes are born of necessity and turn out to be a great hit – a sort of culinary accident – and meatloaf is indeed one of those; we used to trim all our sirloins and then cut them to the desired weight, as I am very fussy about well trimmed steaks. We ended up with a lot of trim, which we minced and had to put to good use. Enter the meatloaf and also a load of other recipes that we call the 'Mince Files', but the meatloaf was always the favourite.

serves 4–5

750g minced beef
175g minced bacon
1 egg beaten
I onion finely chopped
2 cloves garlic crushed
I tblsp each of coriander, parsley and thyme, chopped
100g breadcrumbs
1 tblsp each of the following – tomato ketchup, Worcester sauce, English mustard, Ketjap Manis [or soy sauce]
salt and pepper

Combine all the ingredients in a large mixing bowl and mix thoroughly.

If you want to test for correct seasoning make a little patty, fry it off and then adjust your mix accordingly.

Line a loaf tin with foil and parchment paper, like the terrine on pages 36–37, with enough paper to fold over the top.

Cook for about 2 hours at 180ºC in a bain marie of water in a roasting tin – the water must come at least half way up the loaf tin.

Once it is out of the oven, let it stand for about 10 mins and it will be easier to slice and serve.

This is real comfort food and we like to serve it with mash and onion gravy.

There is a little bonus with this recipe as you can turn the raw mix into very acceptable meatballs with the addition of a little grated parmesan to the mix.

Chicken with curry cream and pilau rice

serves 4

1 onion, sliced
1 clove garlic, crushed
1 heaped dsp of Madras curry paste
250ml chicken stock
250ml double cream
1 tblsp mango chutney
oil
4 chicken breasts

Sauté the onions and garlic, add the curry paste and cook for 5 mins. Add the chicken stock, bring to the boil and add the cream and mango chutney to taste. You are looking for a subtle effect, not heavy on the curry, but with the fruity edge of the mango.

Purée the sauce and thicken it if necessary.

Cut up the chicken and sealin a pan and cook in the sauce for 20 mins. Ensure the chicken is cooked right through and serve.

This dish would be nice served with pan fried okra.

pilau rice

400g rice
2 tblsp oil butter
4 green cardamom pods
4 cloves
50mm cinnamon bark
1 tsp cumin seeds
1 small onion, peeled and sliced
1 tsp salt
1 lt boiling water

This is great served with pilau rice. This recipe is stolen from a wonderful book called *Brit Spice* by Manju Malhi.

Heat the oil in a pan with a lid.

Put in cardamoms, cloves, cinnamon and cumin. Stir for a second or two and then add the onion. Fry for 5 mins then tip in the rice. Add the salt and stir for 30 secs. Add 1 litre boiling water and simmer with the lid on for 8 mins.

Do not lift the lid while cooking as the steam is part of the process.

Peanut and pepper chicken

This is just such a great combination of flavours that occurs in various cuisines around the world. My first encounter with it was that my dad loved it in the guise of West African groundnut stew and then in a slightly spicier manifestation as a satay sauce.

serves 4

either 1 whole chicken, breasts or jointed chicken pieces
1 onion, chopped
3 cloves garlic, crushed
40g root ginger, peeled and cut into slices
1 green and 1 red pepper, deseeded and sliced
1 large green chilli, deseeded and chopped
300g crunchy peanut butter
oil
750 ml chicken stock

Depending on your preference you can joint a whole chicken and seal it in a frying pan and then cook it in the sauce in the oven. Or you can just buy the breasts of chicken and cook them separately and serve with the sauce. My personal preference is for jointed chicken pieces.

Put oil in a saucepan and sweat off the onions and garlic until soft then add the ginger, peppers and chilli, cooking for 5 mins. Now add the peanut butter and the chicken stock. If the sauce is too thick add more stock. Cook the sauce for about 20 mins. If you prefer a smooth sauce you can purée it in a blender.

You can make it into a casserole by sealing off the portions of chicken in a frying pan, then putting them into a casserole dish. Cover with the sauce and bake in an oven at 170°C for 45 mins.

Alternatively you can roast chicken breasts separately and serve the sauce over them.

Best served with some basmati rice.

Hot plum sauce
with chicken or duck – take your pick

My collaborator Jenny McCrea said this had to be in the book and although some people don't like fruit with savoury foods – I just love it.

serves 4

450g fresh plums or if stuck you can use tinned ones
1 red chilli deseeded
I clove garlic, crushed
chicken stock 500ml
2 dsp sugar
1 tblsp soy sauce

4 chicken breasts or boneless thighs –160g per person

Stew the plums with all the other ingredients.
When cooked remove the stones from the plums then blitz all the juice and the stewed plums together.

Use either breast or boneless thighs which have great flavour although people seem obsessed with white meat I think they are missing out.

Marinade the chicken in soy sauce – I like the Indonesian ketjap manis (Asian supermarket) with some vegetable oil and a little lime juice. Leave the skin on the chicken as it protects it while roasting and imparts flavour. It should also go nice and crispy when roasted. You can always leave it on your plate if you are being healthy.

You can make the sauce in advance and just heat it up when you have the chicken cooked.

Put the marinated chicken in a roasting pan and cook in the oven at 180°C for about 20–25 mins.

Serve with boiled rice and a crunchy salad. The sauce can be used like a dip or just poured over the chicken.

Hake baked in a pepperonata sauce

Aka 'spetse fish' after a small island in the Saronic Gulf, Greece, where Kathy and I had our honeymoon 7 months late, but we were skint and had to save up after the event! We had a great couple of weeks. Kathy learned the finer points of ouzo drinking and I learned to love octopus and spetse fish. When we got back home I tried many times to replicate the dish, as experienced on Spetse, and eventually succeeded .

pepperonata sauce	serves 4
1 onion sliced pinch of chilli flakes 1 of each red, green, yellow peppers, sliced 2 fresh tomatoes chopped (you can use tinned in winter) 3 cloves garlic crushed 1 tblsp basil chopped 1 tblsp dill chopped 375cl white wine oil, salt, pepper, sugar tomato ketchup	Heat the oil in a heavy saucepan. Add the onions, garlic and chilli flakes, soften and then add the peppers. Cook for 5 mins, then add the tomatoes, herbs and white wine. Cook for 30 mins and season with salt and pepper then add a little tomato ketchup to give sweetness and balance.
4 pieces of thick hake about 170g per portion	Put a layer of sauce into a pyrex dish followed by the fish and then another layer of sauce. Cover with foil or a lid and bake for about 20 mins. To be authentic serve with sauté potatoes and maybe a greek salad – tomatoes, cucumber, feta red onion olives.

Hake with a tomato and fennel seed sauce

I love hake. We use it a lot although I do realise it is hard to come by. Try Walter Ewing beside the Shankill Leisure Centre or East Coast Seafoods down in Ballyhornan on the old RAF base. If you live in Belfast the market at St Georges sells good fish on Fridays and Saturdays.

Fresh tomato and fennel seed sauce

serves 6

2 onions sliced
2 garlic cloves crushed
560g fresh plum tomatoes chopped
3.5 lt fish stock or chicken stock
2 tblsp fennel seeds
1 level tblsp tomato purée
1 tsp chilli flakes
sugar
olive oil
450g baby spinach
butter
fennel leaves to garnish
fillets of hake – approx. 170g per person

Put the oil into the pan, sweat off the onions and garlic to soften. Add the tomato purée and cook for 2 mins, then add the chopped fresh tomatoes, chilli flakes and cook for 5 mins. Add the stock, cook for about 20 mins and pass the mixture through a sieve. Adjust the seasoning with sugar, salt and pepper.

Put the fennel seeds into a dry frying pan and cook over a high heat for 3 mins. If you need to thicken the sauce use a little cornflour mixed with water and whisk into the simmering liquid.

Season the hake fillet with salt and freshly ground black pepper. Dunk in some olive oil and grill skin up, till cooked.

Melt the butter in a saucepan and just wilt the spinach. Season with salt and pepper.

Assemble on a plate by saucing the plate. Drain the spinach well (you don't want it to leak into your red sauce), place it in the middle of the plate with the hake fillet on top. Garnish with fennel fronds.

Great Italian colours!

Fried spiced monkfish
with a soy and ginger dressing

This is for my friend Maxine Nelson, the MD of our joint venture wine company – in reality she and the team in Hillsborough do all the work and I enjoy the wine. Anyway, she loves this dish and says we never serve it these days. She is probably right, I just know that monkfish is incredibly popular and we usually can't keep it in the house.

A trip to the Chinese supermarket is suggested to get the Asian ingredients.

serves 4

700g monkfish fillets
150g cornflour
30g 5 spice seasoning
1 tsp cayenne
salt and pepper
deep fat fryer or enough oil to fry the fish in

Prepare the fish so you just have a nice fillet without any sinew or bits of cartilage, by cutting into slices about 4mm thick.

Mix up the cornflour, 5 spice, salt and pepper.

Toss the fish in the seasoned flour just before you are ready to cook it.

the dressing

2 tblsp pickled ginger
3 cloves garlic
1 tblsp fish sauce
3 tblsp Ketjap Manis soy sauce
2 tblsp Yeos sweet chilli sauce
2 tblsp sesame oil
2 stalks well trimmed lemon grass
4 lime leaves, sliced with centre removed
20g fresh mint and coriander leaves
1 tblsp rice wine or wine vinegar

Blitz up the ginger, garlic, chilli and lemon grass to a paste in a food processor or blender.

Add the fish sauce and ketup manis and season to taste. May need a little sugar to get the balance right or some lime lemon juice.

We normally serve this on a bed of noodles tossed in the dressing.

Cod (or Pollock) with a chorizo and chickpea stew

Okay, this may not be the most Northern Irish inspired dish you ever met but the influences that Spain has had on my cooking and general gastronomy are immense and this dish is just a wonderful expression of all those robust flavours we have at Nick's.

serves 4

170g of cod per person
1 onion, sliced
3 cloves garlic, crushed
4 plum tomatoes
½ tsp chilli flakes
70g fresh chorizo sliced
pinch of saffron soaked in hot water
sugar, salt and pepper
250ml chickpea stock
oil for frying
1 tsp cumin
2 sprigs rosemary

Soak the raw chickpeas overnight in lots of water and next day cook without salt in boiling water until soft but not falling apart. Just before the end add some salt and make sure to keep the liquid from the cooking!

Heat the oil and cook the chorizo. Add the cumin and chilli flakes to flavour. Now add the onions and garlic, soften and then add the tomatoes. Add the saffron and the stock allowing to simmer for half-an-hour, then season with salt, pepper and a little sugar to balance the dish.

Season the cod with olive oil, salt and pepper and grill skin side up for about 4–5 mins.

To serve, place the cooked cod on top of the chickpea casserole.

Fillet of brill (or turbot or halibut)
with fresh mussels and an anise beurre blanc

Beurre blanc – to some a tricky sauce to make but the secret is good fish stock with some mussel stock mixed in for flavour and unsalted butter. I made this for 'Great British Menu' and whilst everyone loved it I think it just wasn't modern or sexy enough to 'do the business'. Age may not have been on my side either and the talented Danny Miller got through, as he did again in 2009.

100ml mussel liquor (from cooking mussels with onion garlic white wine – see p. 31)
250g unsalted butter
100ml double cream
salt and pepper
1 tsp of pernod
170g brill, turbot or halibut per person

Put the mussel stock and cream into a stainless steel saucepan and bring to the boil. Reduce to about half the original volume and then over a low heat start beating in the unsalted butter with a whisk until all the stock is absorbed and the sauce is glossy and thick. Don't let it boil as it will split. Now add the pernod and check the seasoning.

Season the fish with salt, pepper and melted butter and grill skin side up until cooked.

fishcakes

400g cooked mixed fish
400g potato, cooked and mashed
150g peas defrosted
2 tblsp chopped dill
2 tblsp grain mustard
2 tblsp tomato ketchup
salt and pepper
200g plain flour
400g breadcrumbs
300ml milk
2 eggs

In a large bowl combine the cooked fish with the potato and the other ingredients, season to taste.

Form into little patties, quite flat, so when you cook them they heat through easily. Allow to set in the fridge for at least an hour.

Then set up your breading line – 3 containers, one with flour, one with the eggs and milk beaten up together, and finally one with the breadcrumbs. Put the cakes first in the flour then in the egg mixture making sure you have no dry floury bits showing.

Next roll in the breadcrumbs ensuring they are well covered then place on a tray in the fridge to set for about an hour.

To cook either shallow fry in a frying pan or deep fry. You could be healthy and cook in the oven but I don't think the result will be as good.

We serve with a homemade tartare sauce – just mayonnaise mixed with chopped onion, parsley capers and gherkins.

Thai-style crab cakes

These are all fish with no potato and you make them much smaller than the fishcakes.

serves 5–6

350g white fish
1 tblsp fish sauce
1 tblsp Thai green curry paste
I Keffir lime leaf centre removed and leaf chopped
I tblsp chopped coriander
200g white crab meat (picked over to remove any shell)
50g green beans chopped and blanched
pinch sugar

Put the white fish, fish sauce, curry paste, lime leaf, sugar and coriander into the bowl of a food processor, blitz for about a minute until you have a fishy paste.

Remove from the food processor and put into a bowl. Add the beans and the crab meat and gently incorporate the crab and beans into the mix. The idea being to keep the crab in chunks if possible.

Form into little patties.
Quite small as you are going to serve 2–3 as a starter portion.

To cook shallow fry with a little oil in a frying pan till golden. Brown on both sides. Serve with a dipping sauce.

dipping sauce

3 tblsp Ketjap Manis soy sauce
juice of a lime
1 clove garlic crushed
2 tblsp pickled ginger sliced
2 chillis sliced
sugar to taste

Mix all the ingredients together in a bowl and stir.

fish

Salmon with a dill butter sauce

Salmon – how have you changed? Once upon a time it was plentiful and servants had agreements not to be served it as a staple diet! But we have fished it to death and now, love it or hate it, we have farmed salmon which like all things has its good and bad sides. This is my 'default' fish dish.

It has a great sauce which is easy to make and complements not just salmon but many other fish simply grilled. For variation, use a different herb like sorrel, watercress or tarragon or … what you will!

sauce	serves 6

sauce

small bag fresh dill
1 dsp sugar
1 tblsp vinegar
2 egg yolks
500g melted butter
salt and pepper

fillet of salmon skin on – 170g portion
oil

serves 6

First melt the butter, skim the froth off the top and set aside.

In a food processor whizz up the dill, add the sugar, vinegar and egg yolks, whizz again and, with motor running, slowly add the butter – 'oil' if too thick – add a little hot water. Season.

Grill or fry the salmon, turning once. Don't overcook, about 4–5 mins in total should suffice. Turn once only.

Serve the sauce over the fish and would taste great with new potatoes and fresh asparagus.

One day we asked Walter Ewing, who has a wonderful fish shop on the Shankill, to smoke us some mackerel, not the hot smoked variety that we all know so well, but cold smoked.
This works best when the mackerel is fat and oily and is a completely different texture to the cooked variety.

You can of course substitute fresh, very fresh, mackerel.

Grilled 'cold smoked' mackerel

with a warm salad of asparagus and new potatoes with a dill vinaigrette and horseradish dressing

dill vinaigrette

2 tblsp fresh chopped dill
1 tblsp English mustard
1 dsp of sugar
75ml white wine vinegar
350ml sunflower oil
salt and pepper

serves 4 as a main course

Put the mustard, dill, sugar and vinegar into a glass jar. Put on the top and shake well, adding the oil a little at a time. Each time you add some more oil shake to emulsify, and if it gets too thick, add a tablespoon of water and shake again.

Season to taste with salt and freshly ground black pepper.

horseradish dressing

3 tblsp horseradish root (alternatively the best prepared horseradish sauce)
3 tblsp mayonnaise
2 tblsp double cream

If you can get fresh horseradish root, peel and grate about 3 tablespoonfuls of it into a bowl. Add the mayonnaise and double cream.

Mix all together and create a reasonably firm sauce. If you are unable to source fresh horseradish (which is very hot) use the very best prepared horseradish you can get and add cream to it.

4 mackerel boned out and trimmed into fillets
oil for grilling
salt and pepper
allow 4–5 potatoes and about 6 spears of asparagus per person.

Cook the potatoes and asparagus in separate pans of salted boiling water, taking care not overcook the asparagus.

Once cooked, reserve, and keep warm. The potatoes will take 15–20 mins and the asparagus about ¾ of a minute.

Now grill the mackerel, brushed with oil, until just cooked.

to assemble

Cut the warm potatoes and asparagus spears in half. Toss together in a bowl with the dill vinaigrette and put onto the serving plate with the mackerel on top. Dot the rim of the plate with the horseradish dressing and garnish with fresh dill.

In the early days, we used to serve the new season asparagus as then it was a real treat and seasonal unlike the all year round stuff we get now. But people didn't really know how to eat it and frequently we would get plates back into the kitchen with a neat row of asparagus tips left on the plate, i.e they had missed the best bit – dilemma: how do you tell them – warning eat sharp end first? It used to amaze a French waiter we had at the time: 'oh les Irlandais'!

vegetarian

Nut loaf

This delicious default veggie dish is great if you have a carnivorous friend to feed.

Any nuts will do but I always include cashews and avoid walnuts as they impart a bitter taste. In the cook offs we discovered that it went brilliantly with the curry cream sauce – pure serendipity.

serves 4–5

1 onion diced
2 cloves garlic crushed
200g cashews
100g hazelnuts
100g brazil nuts
60g breadcrumbs
200ml vegetable stock
oil/butter
2 tblsp mixed herbs, chopped or
1 dsp dried
salt and pepper

Sweat the onion, garlic and herbs in oil to soften, then put into the food processor with the mixed nuts, and blitz lightly.

You want the nuts to retain a bit of shape and texture. Remove from the processor and put into a large bowl with the breadcrumbs.

Mix thoroughly. Now slowly add the vegetable stock to bind the mixture. It should be moist but not sloppy.

Taste and season the mixture.

Put into a greased loaf tin and bake in an oven at 190ºC for 1 hour.

options

You can season with soy sauce.

Add mushrooms which have been fried with the onions and garlic.

Chestnut stuffed cabbage

A tasty filling veggie dish that I think we first used one Christmas – it looks great on the plate.

serves 4

100g dried chestnuts
1 small savoy cabbage
25g butter
1 clove garlic, crushed
100g leeks
100g mushrooms, dried
2 tsp lemon juice
2 tsp paprika
2 tsp dill
1 egg
salt and pepper

Soak the chestnuts in hot water for an hour or longer, then cook in the liquid for about 40 mins until soft, drain and chop up the chestnuts.

Unwrap the outer leaves of the cabbage and trim out the hard white stalk up the middle in a v shape. Blanch for 2 mins in boiling water. Then finely chop the rest of the cabbage.

Melt the butter in a frying pan and sweat off the garlic, leeks, mushrooms and chopped cabbage over a low heat for 7–10 mins. Add the chestnuts, lemon juice, dill and paprika. Allow to cool, then mix in the egg, and season well.

Line a greased pudding basin with the blanched cabbage leaves leaving enough to fold over the top when full. Spoon in the chestnut mixture and cover with the leaves, put a plate on top to weigh it down and bake for an hour.

Great with fresh tomato and fennel sauce – see page 76.

Spinach and lentil timbales

I dreamt these up as I wanted to have a dish for vegetarians that we could cook to order so it is designed to be cooked in a microwave. I did try it in the oven when recipe testing but it didn't work as well.

serves 4

1 onion finely chopped
1 clove garlic crushed
225g spinach wilted in butter
160g cooked green lentils
1 egg
seasoning: 1 tblsp chopped marjoram or herb of your choice
60g soft melting cheese like fontina or Comté or even hard sheep cheese
50g breadcrumbs
butter

Melt the butter in a pan, sweat the onion and garlic then add the spinach. Now put that mixture into a food processor with the breadcrumbs, herbs and the egg.

Blitz the mixture, then fold in the lentils and the grated melting cheese. These are designed to be cooked in a greased ramekin in the microwave for about 1½ mins.

It is lovely and moist.

Serve with some boiled potatoes and maybe a little ratatouille. I did try cooking in the oven but it didn't work as well.

As a variation you could grill some portabella mushrooms with butter and use them instead of the ramekins, or cook the mushrooms and turn the ramekins out on top.

A butter sauce like the one on page 81 might go well with this dish.

Spinach and filo pie

Inspired by the greek dish spanakopita.

This is a dual purpose recipe because if you substitute parmesan for the feta you have a great filling for canneloni – though it would also work if you kept the feta in!

serves 4

Ingredients	Method
filo pastry 225g fresh spinach wilted in butter 125g ricotta cheese 250g feta cheese 2 eggs 250g melted butter 1 tblsp dill, chopped oil 1 large onion chopped 2 cloves garlic crushed salt and pepper	Soften the onions and garlic in the oil. Add the spinach and just wilt it. Now drain very thoroughly to get rid of all the water in the spinach. Put this mixture into a food processor and blitz with the cheeses, the eggs and the chopped dill, check the seasoning. In a rectangular dish – at work we use a swiss roll tin or a roasting tray – layer up 3 sheets of filo pastry brushing each layer with melted butter as you go. Bake for about 15 mins to a golden brown then remove from the oven and cover with a layer of spinach mixture. Then, add a further 3 buttered layers of filo, return to the oven and bake for about 30–40mins until golden brown Served with tomato and fennel sauce – see page 76.

Canneloni with spinach and cheese filling

serves 4–6

Ingredients	Method
225g fresh spinach wilted in butter 125g ricotta cheese 250g feta cheese – substitute parmesan if preferred 2 eggs 250g melted butter 1 tblsp dill, chopped oil 1 large onion chopped 2 cloves garlic crushed salt and pepper	First make a cheese sauce – see page 64. Next, fill the cannelloni tubes with the spinach and cheese of choice mixture. Then, in a deep ovenproof dish, put a layer of sauce followed by the filled cannelloni and finally another layer of sauce. Bake at 180°C for 45 mins. Allow 4 canneloni per person. The canneloni is also good made with the meat sauce from the lasagne on page 64 as an alternative to the cheese sauce.

Chickpea tagine with couscous

Chickpeas to me always taste better if you cook them yourself. I realise this is tedious and it's much easier to open a tin but the stock that you get from cooking your own more than rewards the effort. So …

tagine

serves 4

1 onion peeled and sliced
3 cloves garlic crushed
2 carrots peeled and chopped
2 peppers sliced
3 sticks celery peeled and chopped
1 aubergine cubed and fried in hot oil until soft
tagine spice (1 dsp coriander seed, cumin seed, mustard seed, roasted and ground 2.5cm of cinnamon bark)
tomato purée
vegetable stock (from chickpeas)
250g chickpeas soaked and cooked
6 dried apricots, chopped
oil

Soak the dried chickpeas overnight, cook in the soaking water, then top up to cover. Do not add any salt at this stage as it makes them tough. Cook until they are as soft as you like them, which can take 40 mins. It will form a white scum on top – just skim it off, season with salt at the end of cooking and keep the cooking liquor. This method can be used for most beans with a similar great result.

Sweat the onions and garlic in the oil, now add the peppers, carrots and celery. Sweat for 3–4 mins. Now add the tagine spice and cook out. Then add the tomato purée and mix in well.

Next, add the stock, the chickpeas and the cooked aubergines. Finally the chopped dried apricots. Allow to simmer for about 30 mins.

Taste and correct seasoning; it may need lemon juice or a little sugar to balance the sweet/sour nature of the dish.

the couscous

250g couscous
25g fresh mint chopped
25g fresh parsley chopped
1 onion chopped and fried
25g raisins
25g pinenuts or sunflower seeds
salt and pepper

Soak the couscous in a large bowl of cold water. This makes it light and separates the grains. Let it stand for 30 mins. Now add the chopped onion, the herbs and the raisins. Don't stint on the herbs.

Season with salt and pepper.

We sometimes toss the sunflower seeds/pinenuts in soy sauce and grill them to add into the couscous, however, that may be too cross cultural for you, but is very tasty!

■ vegetarian ■

Side orders

Spiced cauliflower

This dish gives the humble cauliflower a whole new persona and at home
I am guilty of serving it constantly!

serves 4–5

1 large cauliflower
2.5cm fresh ginger, peeled
1 green chilli, chopped – deseeded if you
don't like it too hot
4 tblsp vegetable oil
salt
1 tsp sugar
1 tsp coriander seeds
2 tsp mustard seeds
1 tsp cumin seeds
2 tblsp fresh lemon juice
chopped coriander or parsley leaves
2 cloves garlic

Cut the cauliflower into florets.

In a heavy pan dry fry the cumin, coriander, and mustard seeds.
Then add the oil, chilli, ginger and garlic. Now add the cauliflower
salt, sugar and lemon juice.

Make sure you have enough liquid to steam the cauliflower with
the lid on for about 15 mins. I like it to have a bit of bite. Check on
it after 6–7 mins. Cook longer if you like a softer vegetable.

Sprinkle with fresh coriander or parsley before serving.

Celeriac mash

Celeriac is such a versatile vegetable: it's great in soups and is also good cold grated with carrot say, and a dressing, vinaigrette or mayonnaise.

serves 4

1kg peeled potatoes cooked, ready to mash

1 large celeriac cooked and puréed with cream

butter

cream

salt and pepper

Put the drained boiled potatoes into the pan, add the warm puréed celeriac and mash well together.

Season with butter, cream, salt and pepper, or you can just blitz the celeriac in a food processor, and add into the potatoes.

Don't be tempted to put the potatoes into the food processor as it will change texture and become unpleasant.

Swede or turnip

Anyway, I mean the yellow/orange fleshed root vegetable that we used to feed our sheep.

Here are two cooking options.

serves 4

Simply peel the swede and cut into chunks.

Cook in boiling salted water until soft.

1 swede/turnip

100ml double cream

salt and pepper

100g butter

Plan A: purée in a food processor with the addition of double cream, butter, salt and pepper – it really elevates this great cheap vegetable to a new level!

1 swede/turnip

2 tblsp mayonnaise

salt and pepper

100g breadcrumbs

2 cloves garlic chopped

butter/oil

Plan B: toss in mayonnaise and sprinkle with breadcrumbs that you have fried with chopped garlic. Your guests will all wonder how you made this!

Beetroot and horseradish bake

I fed this to my mother-in-law about thirty years ago and she still thinks it's
one of the best things I have ever given her to eat!

serves 4 as a side dish

50g butter
50g flour
400ml milk hot
4 roasted beetroot, peeled
and sliced – see recipe for dip page 24
1 onion sliced
Flavour with either fresh horseradish or
the best quality preserved horseradish
you can get – Tracklements is one to look
out for in a deli.

Melt the butter, add the flour and cook gently over a low heat until you achieve a sandy texture. It is important to get rid of the floury taste now. Gradually add the hot milk, beating vigorously as you go, and once a smooth texture has been achieved, add in the horseradish and season with salt and pepper.

Pour a layer of sauce into a deep ceramic or metal dish. Add a layer of beetroot, a layer of onion, then more sauce and repeat the process.

Now bake in the oven at 170°C for about 40 mins or until good and hot with a brown top – very tasty: 'beetrootophobes' will love it.

Pommes anna

Impressive and quite cheffy looking, but not that difficult to make. Season well.

serves 6

250g floury potatoes sliced
thinly in a mandolin
50g butter
salt and pepper

Put 25g butter into a heavy 20cm frying pan with sloping sides and melt over a moderate heat. Then layer the potato slices in the pan neatly, overlapping them to form the base layer, which will be the top when you have finished.

Now layer the rest of the potatoes, seasoning as you go.

Finally dot the top with the remaining 25g butter and bake for an hour at 220°C.

To serve, turn the pan upside down onto a plate and cut into wedges.

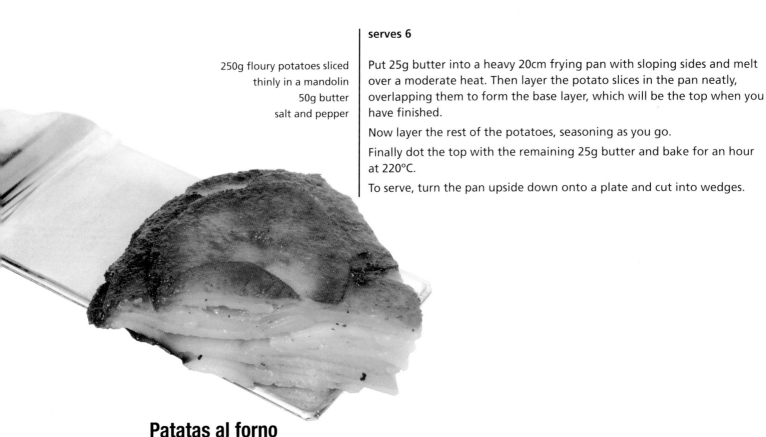

Patatas al forno

This dish is a little similar to pommes anna, but we normally make it in a roasting tray and use olive oil instead of butter, and add rosemary.

serves 6

250g potatoes
olive oil
salt and pepper
fresh rosemary

Slice the potatoes on a mandolin or very thinly by hand or even mechanically.

Grease the tin with olive oil and layer up the potatoes, seasoning each layer with salt, pepper and chopped rosemary.

Brush each layer with olive oil up to the top. Then put the tin into the oven and bake for 1 hour. The top should be nice and brown and crunchy.

Carrots with lemon and parsley

It's a great delight that my son Ben's partner Danielle loves food. She picked the right family. This is Granny Price's recipe for carrots and we all love it, but you have to get the carrots before Danielle does!

quantity of small sweet carrots

Not really a recipe but simply a great way to serve carrots. Best with small sweet carrots, I buy the ones with the tops on.

Peel and cook the carrots in boiling salted water, drain and add butter, black pepper, chopped parsley and fresh lemon juice.

Cabbage casserole

Whenever we make this, people just love it. The trick is to leave the cabbage crunchy, the nuts and raisins are optional but provide taste explosions.

serves 4–6

1 small round cabbage, sliced quite finely, as for coleslaw
2 carrots, peeled and grated
1 large onion, sliced
mix all these together in a bowl

1 cooking apple, made into a sweet apple sauce (or use a bought jar!)
1 small packet salted peanuts
1 small handful of raisins
salt and pepper

Melt 20g of butter with some oil in a saucepan (sesame oil is good).

Add the vegetables and stir to coat them all with the oil.

Turn down the heat to a simmer and put the lid on. Return to stir the veg every few minutes to prevent sticking, and if they are sticking, add a small quantity of water.

Cook until they are al dente, depending on taste, and then add the apple sauce, nuts and raisins, and season.

Dauphinoise potatoes

Choose a dish to cook these in that can go on top of the stove as well as in the oven. We have always found that this recipe works best done this way and the potatoes discolour least if you bring them up to a good temperature fast on a top ring. Waxy potatoes are best for this dish.

serves 6

good white potatoes, peeled and sliced into 50mm rings
2 large onions, sliced
4 cloves garlic, peeled and squashed
100g butter
250ml full fat milk
250ml whipping cream
grated cheese
salt and pepper

Dot a bit of the butter on the bottom of the chosen dish, and then start layering alternately with potato and onion, adding garlic, butter, salt and pepper with each layer. I know salt is the enemy, but this is one dish that really benefits from good seasoning, as the milk and cream can seem very bland without it.

Pour on the milk and put the dish on the top plate, bring to the boil, but do not let the bottom layer burn. Now pour on the cream and sprinkle the cheese over the top and put into the oven at 180°C for about 30 mins, until the potatoes are cooked and the top is golden brown.

There are many variations on this dauphinoise recipe. It is delicious with potatoes and Jerusalem artichokes, celeriac, or even swedes/turnips.

The cheese can be replaced by toasted buttery breadcrumbs for crunch.

Boulangère potatoes

Boulangère potatoes get their name from the habit in France of locals making use of the bakers oven after he had baked for the day, using the residual heat to cook various dishes back in the days when people didn't have ovens. This works in much the same way as Dauphinoise potatoes, except, instead of all those politically incorrect dairy products, stock is used!

serves 6

a quantity of good white potatoes, sliced into 50mm rings
2 onions sliced to layer with the potatoes
garlic as desired
grated cheese for the topping
500ml good stock, either beef or chicken, depending on what you are serving them with

Having layered the potatoes and onions, pour on the stock and bring to the boil on top of the cooker, then sprinkle with the cheese and bake in the oven at 180°C until cooked through and golden brown on top.

sauces

Customers have always liked our sauces and most of them are easy to make! Enjoy!

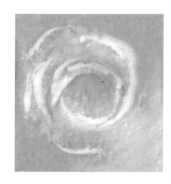

'the saucier's apprentice'

or a brief guide to what sauce goes with what!

CHICKEN	PORK	BEEF	VENISON	LAMB
mushroom cream	mushroom cream	mushroom cream	port & green peppercorn	port & green peppercorn
port & green peppercorn	port & green peppercorn	port & green peppercorn	red wine	honey & ginger
honey & ginger	honey & ginger	grain mustard	five spice	red wine
red pepper & pimenton	grain mustard	guinness & oyster	red wine & lentils	red wine & lentils
grain mustard	five spice	red wine		five spice
five spice	curry cream	red wine & lentils		chickpea tagine
basil pesto	hot plum	chorizo & chickpea stew		

			FISH	DUCK
curry cream	peanut & pepper		chorizo & chickpea stew	port & green peppercorn
hot plum	parmigani		tomato & fennel	honey & ginger
peanut & pepper	tomato & fennel		pepperonata sauce	red wine
parmigani			beurre blanc	red wine & lentils
tomato & fennel			dill and butter sauce	hot plum
pepperonata sauce				five spice
chorizo & chickpea stew				

Wild mushroom cream sauce

In a perfect world, you go out to the woods in the autumn and gather ceps and saffron milk caps to make this sauce, but in the real world, you can improvise with dried ceps, and whatever fresh mushrooms you can get. So it can be a mixture of shitake, chestnut, oyster and for flavour dried ceps soaked in boiling water.

serves 5–6

butter
1 medium onion chopped
1 clove garlic crushed
120g mixed mushrooms + 1 small packet
dried ceps soaked in boiling water
300ml white wine
300ml chicken stock
200ml double cream

Melt the butter and sauté the onion and garlic till soft.

Add the fresh mixed mushrooms and cook for 5 mins. Now add the soaked ceps and the soaking water. Be careful not to use the sediment as it may be a bit earthy.

Now add the white wine and let that cook for 5 mins to boil off the alcohol. Next, add the stock and the cream and cook for a further 20mins.

Taste, adjust the seasoning and thicken if necessary.

Honey and ginger sauce

I think this recipe originally came from the Miller Howe in the Lake District, but it is such a long time ago I can't remember. It is very adaptable and we serve it with quail, chicken and pork.

sauce for 6

oil
1 onion peeled and finely chopped
1 clove garlic
2 dsp curry paste
I tblsp tomato purée
3 tbls honey
130g root ginger ½ coarsely chopped
and ½ peeled and cut into matchsticks
500ml chicken stock
3 tblsp soy sauce/Ketjap Manis

In a saucepan sweat off the onions and garlic over a low heat then add the curry paste and cook out for 3–4 mins. Next add the tomato purée, mix in well and cook for a further 3 mins. Then add the honey, chicken stock and coarsely chopped ginger.

Simmer for 20 mins gently as it has a tendency to boil over. Strain the sauce, add in the matchsticks of ginger and simmer for a further 15 mins.

Adjust the seasoning with lemon juice and thicken.

Port and green peppercorn sauce

I love this sauce: it works best with red meats lamb in particular and venison.

sauce for 6

1 onion, finely chopped
1 tsp chilli powder
1tblsp tomato purée
300ml ruby port
750ml lamb or chicken stock
1 large sprig of rosemary
1 tblsp redcurrant jelly
1 tblsp green peppercorns in brine
well rinsed!
butter or oil
salt pepper

In a saucepan over a moderate heat, sweat off the onion to soften in oil or butter. Next, add the chilli powder and cook off for 3 mins. Then add the tomato purée, mix in well and add the port.

Flambé the port to burn off the alcohol – watch your eyebrows! Then add the stock, rosemary and redcurrant jelly.

Simmer for 20 mins and then strain the sauce.

Add in the well rinsed green peppercorns, bring back to the boil and taste the sauce. It may need a little more redcurrant jelly, also, thicken as desired.

Red pepper and pimenton sauce

This is a rich and robust sauce with strong flavours of Spain, the home of some of my most favourite gastronomic experiences in the last few years.

sauce for 6

olive oil
3 cloves crushed garlic
4 red peppers sliced or (you can cheat and use the jars of grilled red peppers)
I dsp Pimenton (use the dolce as the hot one is very, very hot)
375ml white wine
2 chicken stock cubes
390g tomato passata
salt, pepper and sugar

Put olive oil in a saucepan, sweat off the onion and garlic.

Soften over a low heat then add the red peppers and the pimenton. Continue to cook over a low heat for a further 10 mins, cook for another 2–3 mins, then add the white wine.

Turn up the heat and boil off the alcohol.

Now add the stock and the crushed tomatoes, simmer for a further 20 mins. Check and adjust seasoning. Now liquidise the sauce and it is ready to use.

Great with grilled chicken or fish.

Grain mustard sauce

This is a very versatile sauce as it is complementary to lots of dishes like pork, fish or maybe even gammon or steak. We like to serve it with colcannon mash and loin of rare breed pork. Oh, and you can coat your steak in mustard seeds and grill it, serve it with the sauce – brill!

sauce for 6

butter or oil
2 medium onion chopped finely
2 tblsp English mustard
40g yellow mustard seeds
200ml white wine
200ml chicken stock
250ml cream
1 tblsp grain mustard
salt, pepper and sugar

In a dry pan fry the mustard seeds. Set aside in a bowl then sauté the onion to soften in the melted butter or oil. Next, add the English mustard and cook gently for 5 mins.

Add the white wine and cook out the alcohol for a further 5 mins then add the stock and finally the cream. Cook for a further 20 mins.

Then add the grain mustard and the seeds. Season with salt and pepper. It may need a little sugar, and add more English mustard and thicken as you see fit.

Guinness and oyster sauce

Once upon a time I was foolish enough to think that I invented this dish but in fact it's merely an interpretation of a classic idea for a beef casserole. The Guinness and the oysters seem to complement each other beautifully.

sauce for 4

butter
1 onion peeled and sliced
I tblsp chopped parsley
1 tblsp chopped thyme
I tblsp tomato purée
I tin 440ml Guinness
500ml beef stock
150g oyster meat
100g mushroom if liked fried in a little butter
1 carrot peeled and cut into matchsticks
2 celery sticks peeled and cut into matchsticks

In a saucepan melt the butter, then add the onion and chopped herbs until the onions are soft. Next, add the tomato purée and cook for 5 mins.

Now, add the Guinness and simmer for a further 5 mins then add the beef stock and simmer for 30 mins.

Strain out the onions, sauté the mushrooms in a little butter and add mushrooms, carrot, celery and the oyster meats. Cook for a further 10 mins.

Adjust the seasoning and check texture.

We serve this with a nice grilled steak but it is also very good as a braising liquor for slowly cooked braising steak.

Five spice sauce

This sauce was inspired by my love of Chinese cooking and its flavoursome spice mix is not hot [chilli hot]. It works very well with pork, chicken or duck. All the waiting staff are obliged to learn what the 5 spices are as everone always asks; they are – fennel, cardamom, star anise, clove and cinnamon, but we always buy them made up. I have tried some versions that I have bought in supermarkets but they just don't have the depth of flavour I have found in the authentic Chinese supermarket version.

sauce for 4–6

Ingredients	Method
2 onions, sliced	Sweat off the onions in oil until transparent.
3 dsp Chinese 5 spice powder	Add the 5 spice powder and cook for 2–3 mins, stirring constantly.
2 dsp tomato purée	Add tomato purée and repeat. Add the wine and stock.
½ bottle white wine	Simmer for 30 mins, strain the onions out of the sauce and add honey and oyster sauce tasting as you go. Simmer for another 10 mins.
500ml chicken stock	
1 tblsp honey	Thicken with cornflour and water.
oyster sauce	
oil to cook onions	

Red wine sauce

Red wine sauce is only ever as good as its ingredients, and I like to use a robust red wine, a good meat stock and a few sprigs of rosemary.

sauce for 4–6

Ingredients	Method
butter	Melt the butter and sweat off the shallots/onions and garlic until softened; now add the tomato purée and cook for 5 mins on a low heat. Then add the red wine, bringing to a brisk boil to cook off the alcohol for about 5 mins. Then add the stock and the rosemary.
1 onion or shallots, finely chopped	
2 cloves garlic, crushed	
1 tbls tomato purée	
375ml red wine, something gutsy like shiraz	Simmer for about 30 mins, strain out the onions and rosemary and return to the pan checking consistency and seasoning. I sometimes add a little sugar or balsamic vinegar to give an edge to the sauce. Reduce the sauce a bit more if it is not thick enough or add thickening. If you want a really rich glossy sauce whisk a knob of butter in before serving.
500ml well flavoured beef stock	
3 sprigs of rosemary	

I also sometimes add a little redcurrant jelly, but then I have a sweet tooth.

This is essentially a sauce I like to serve with beef, but it is also good with lamb or venison.

Pickles and relishes

NB: chutneys and relishes need to cook slowly and
are quite labour intensive, so get a heat diffuser and
put it under your saucepan to stop the precious
chutney from burning.

It is just heartbreaking and very annoying ….
I know I was that chef!

Basil pesto

We grew a new variety at home this year and the leaves were as big as my hand and quite spicy to taste, but worked well on test.

50g fresh basil
50g pine nuts
50g fresh grated parmesan cheese
2 cloves garlic
200ml olive oil, mild, not too strong
salt and freshly ground black pepper

Put the basil and garlic into the food processor, whizz to chop finely, then add the pine nuts and parmesan cheese. Whizz again to a fine paste, then with the motor running, slowly pour the olive oil down the feed tube, continuing until the sauce binds together – 40 or 50 seconds.

Season to taste. It will need the salt and pepper just to finish it off.

Make sure you get an olive oil that you particularly like, virgin or not, as it is a key ingredient.

variation

You could use a different herb, e.g. coriander, parsley or you could even add a few sun-dried tomatoes.

We serve this mostly with good fresh fillets of fish be it turbot, cod or salmon. It is also great with pasta or just to dunk bread into!

Cranberry relish

I found this one year on a pack of ocean spray cranberries, so made it, and found it amazing and so easy.

It has been Kathy's contribution to Christmas lunch ever since. With three cooks in the family, she figured she was best taking a back seat.

1 whole orange cut into chunks skin and all (remove pips)
500g cranberries
caster sugar to taste

Place cranberries and orange in a food processor and whizz. Add sugar to get a nice tart sweet and sour flavour. Will keep for about two weeks in the fridge.

Rouille

4 cloves garlic, peeled and crushed
1 red chilli, deseeded and chopped
1 large red pepper – grilled and skinned
½ tsb hot pimenton – Spanish smoked paprika
180ml olive oil
2 tbls fresh breadcrumbs

Grill the red pepper, when well charred all round remove from the heat and put in a bowl, cover with clingfilm and leave for 5 mins.

Remove skin, stalk and seeds.

Put the red pepper flesh, chilli, garlic and paprika into the food processor and blitz to a purée, with the motor running, add the olive oil until well incorporated. Finally, add the breadcrumbs and blitz again.

Season with salt and freshly ground black pepper.

Use with the Mediterranean fish soup on a croûton – see page 55 – or with a spicy tomato stew.

Cucumber pickle

A real favourite of mine! This is fab with fish or cheese, and a great way of using up a glut of cucumbers in the greenhouse.

Ingredients	Method
4 large cucumbers 3 medium onions 50g salt	Slice the cucumbers and the onions on a mandolin. Layer them up in a colander, salting each layer, put a plate on top and put a weight on top of the plate to square off the layer. Stand to drain for 3 hours.

Make up the pickle/syrup as follows

Ingredients	Method
570ml white wine vinegar 454g soft brown sugar ½ level tsp ground tumeric ¼ tsp ground cloves 1 tblsp yellow mustard seeds	Put all of the above into a large stainless steel saucepan and heat until the sugar is dissolved. Thoroughly rinse the cucumber and onion under the tap, then drain it. Put into the syrup and bring to boil cooking for 3 mins. Remove with a slotted spoon or sieve. Reduce the syrup by boiling for 15 to 20 mins, then put the cucumber and onion into sterilised jars, and pour the syrup over the top and seal.

Harissa

A great North African seasoning ingredient.

1 tblsp tomato purée
1 tblsp freshly roasted and ground coriander
1 tsp powdered saffron
3 red peppers, deseeded, roasted and skinned
15 green chillis, deseeded
1 tsp cayenne pepper

Put all the ingredints into a food processor and blend.

Caesar dressing

I love a good Caesar salad just a plain one as its inventor intended. I put the anchovies in the dressing as some people don't like them in their salad and they enhance the dressing with flavour but you don't get a mouthful of salty anchovies.

400g mayonnaise – make your own or use the best you can
3 cloves garlic crushed
15g fresh basil
3 salted anchovy fillets
50g fresh parmesan or garana padano grated

Put the garlic, basil, anchovies and parmesan into a food processor and blitz.

Then add the mayonnaise and blitz again. Season with black pepper and, if too thick, add a tablespoonful of water and blitz again.

Serve cos lettuce with some bread croûtons, grated parmesan and the dressing … Voilà!

Vinaigrette

I like to make this in a jam jar with a good lid, and the secret is to add the oil gradually.

30g English mustard
10g sugar
40g cider or white wine vinegar
170g sunflower oil
salt and black pepper

Put the mustard, sugar and vinegar into the jar, and put the lid on: shake vigorously.

Add a third of the oil and shake again and so on until all of the oil is incorporated. If it is too thick, add a tablespoonful of water and shake again. Season. Keep in the fridge in a squeezy bottle, use as required.

Tomato relish

2.3kg tomatoes skinned and chopped
10 green peppers chopped
10 cloves garlic crushed
2.5kg cooking apples peeled and chopped
1.25lt malt vinegar
Then add :
1.75kg sugar
5 tblsp salt
5 tblsp paprika
2.5 tsp cayenne
5 tblsp mustard
2.5 tsp mixed spice
700g tomato purée

Put all the ingredients into a big stainless steel saucepan and simmer for 30 mins.

Then simmer gently for about an hour until you reach the desired consistency.

I find a heat diffuser under the saucepan a very worth while idea as it stops the mixture burning.

Put into sterilised jars and seal.

Mint relish

A great alternative to mint sauce

1.35kg bramley apples
1.35kg onions
450g raisins
zest and juice of 2 lemons
700g brown sugar
570ml malt vinegar
lots of chopped mint
100g yellow mustard seeds

Peel and finely chop the onions and apples.

Put all the ingredients into a large saucepan and simmer until they reach a desired consistency.

relish

Plum chutney

900g plums	Remove stones from the plums. Peel and core the apples. Dice both and place in a pan with chopped onions and all the other ingredients. Simmer for 2–2½ hours stirring occasionally. Bottle while hot into warm sterilised jars. Seal when cold.
900g green apples	
450g onions chopped	
225g raisins	
225g sultanas	
110g preserved ginger	
450g soft brown sugar	
1 tsp cayenne pepper	
2 tblsp salt	
1.4 lt wine vinegar	

Marrow chutney

2.3kg marrow	Peel the marrow, remove seeds and cut into cubes. Salt and leave overnight.
50g salt	
225g onion	Peel and chop all the vegetables, boil the onions in a little water until tender then drain. Rinse the marrow to get rid of the salt and cook all together to desired consistency.
225g each of raisins, sultanas, currants	
225g soft brown sugar	
10g ground ginger	
25g mustard seed	Bottle while hot into warm sterilised jars. Seal when cold.
570ml vinegar	

Mango chutney

2.3kg green mangoes	Peel and chop the mangoes and tomatoes, add all the other ingredients and simmer for an hour on low.
450g firm tomatoes	
900g sliced onions	
900g raisins	
900g soft brown sugar	Store in a sterilised container.
850ml vinegar	
50g chillis	
110g salt	
2 tblsp curry powder or to taste	

Apple and tomato chutney

1kg cooking apples
1kg onions
1kg tomatoes
12.5g mixed pickling spice
200g sultanas
½ lt vinegar
500g black treacle
2 tsp salt
75ml mustard seeds

Peel and core the apples, chop the onions and tomatoes, place in a stainless steel saucepan with all the other ingredients.

Cook gently for approx. 2½ hours.

Store in a sterilised container.

Orange chutney

4 oranges peeled and chopped
2 apples peeled and chopped
1 onion peeled and chopped
110g preserved ginger
10g chillis deseeded and chopped
450g soft brown sugar
110g raisins
570ml vinegar
25g salt
¼ tsp pepper

Mix all the ingredients in a stainless steel saucepan and cook gently for approx. 1 hour.

Store in a sterilised container.

An Irish membrillo!

To serve with cheese or if you have a glut of cooking apples.

1kg prepared cooking apples – peeled cored and grated
1kg preserving sugar
700ml water

Dissolve the sugar in the water in a large saucepan over a moderate heat.

Add the apple and simmer uncovered for at least 2 hours stirring occasionally until it forms a thick solid appearance.

Pour into a loaf tin lined with cling film and allow to set in the fridge.

puddings

Some would say that you have a dessert or a sweet at the end of the meal, but at Nick's we have always just had puddings, be they light or more robust, traditional or modern; they are all very tasty and a terrible temptation to someone who has a sweet tooth like me, no apologies for all the chocolate ones either!

Baked american cheesecake

You could make a sponge base, but for simplicity and ease, best to buy one. Cut it in half and shape into a springform tin, filling the cracks with extra sponge if necessary.

You could freeze the remainder for the next time.

makes 12 portions

225g caster sugar
3tblsp (24g) cornflour
750g cream cheese – we use Fivemiletown cream cheese in the restaurant, but Philly will do just as well or even own brand as long as it's full fat!
2 eggs
1 tsp vanilla essence
300ml whipping cream

Mix the sugar and cornflour and add the cream cheese. Blend to a creamy consistency, then beat in the eggs and vanilla, finally adding the cream to create a thick, creamy consistency.

Beat it really well to aerate as there is an argument in the kitchen that says it is better if you leave this cheese mixture overnight to mature but try it both ways and make up your own mind.

Scoop the mixture onto the sponge base and bake at 180°C for 40–45 mins until it is light brown on top. Run a knife around the rim as soon as it comes out of the oven to prevent it cracking as it cools.

This is really great just as vanilla, but you can incorporate blueberries or cherries very successfully into the mix, however most people seem to prefer a compôte of a sharp flavoured fruit served with it.

Warehouse crumble

Mum used to make the best crumble ever and when I asked her secret she said it was a lot of fat to flour.

serves 6

40g caster sugar
40g soft brown sugar
80g flour
60g butter
700g fruit – apple, banana, plum and blackberry

Soften the butter if mixing by hand, cut into small pieces and mix with the dry ingredients. Alternatively, blitz in the food processor until it resembles rough breadcrumbs. I like it to form a crumbly texture, for this it's best if the butter is hard.

The crumble can be spread over any favourite fruity combination, our most popular at the Warehouse are apple, apple and banana, plum, and apple and blackberry.

I like to bake the filling and then add the crumble topping and sprinkle with a few drops of water.

Bake at 160°C for 30 mins until it turns a pretty golden brown.

It is also possible to cook the crumble separately and then set on top of the fruit purée.

Crème brûlée

serves 5

500ml whipping cream
6 egg yolks
100g caster sugar
1 vanilla pod or 2 tsp vanilla essence
tiny pinch of salt – optional but brings
out vanilla flavour

Put cream into a saucepan with the vanilla and heat to just below boiling point.

In a bowl, whisk by hand the yolks and sugar. Now pour the cream onto the egg and sugar mixture, stirring constantly. If you like the effect of the black vanilla seeds in your brûlée scrape them out and add to the mix.

Now strain the mix in case there are any lumps or pieces of shell.

Pour into individual ramekins trying not to have any air bubbles in the mix. A chef would take a blowtorch and just pass it over the top and it has the effect of bursting the air bubbles. Put these in a roasting tray and fill the tray with warm water, about half way up the ramekin. Cover the tray with foil and bake in the oven for about 30 mins at 140°C. The custard should be just set and no more, check after 15 mins to make sure.

Remove from the tray and allow to set in the fridge overnight.

To serve sprinkle with caster sugar and either grill the tops to form the brûlée or with a blowtorch gradually play the flame on the sugar to create a golden brown crunchy top.

We like to serve these with a seasonal fruit compôte and a little tuile or shortbread biscuit.

Chocolate biscuit cake

serves 6

200g dark chocolate
200g butter
2 eggs
50g caster sugar
200g digestive biscuits

Melt the chocolate with the butter, either gently in the microwave or in a bowl over a pan of simmering water.

Cream the eggs with the sugar and pour over the melted chocolate mixture.

In a large bowl, break 200g of digestive biscuits and pour on the chocolate mix, stirring to cover the biscuits thoroughly.

Pour this knobbly mixture into a well greased springform or loaf tin and chill. Run a knife around the rim before turning out onto a pretty plate.

At the warehouse we sometimes do this with white chocolate which is richer and a whole lot sweeter.

Or you could be really cheffy and do a black and white biscuit cake by making a dark batch and then a white batch on top so effectively you just divide the recipe in half and substitute white for dark chocolate. Use the best white chocolate you can find.

Chocolate guinness cake

This recipe is adapted from one by Nigella Lawson, but I am quite sure we made it long before that. It's just that we didn't used to heat the Guinness and we think that made it curdle.

serves 6–8

400ml guinness
150g dark chocolate
230ml butter
340g soft brown sugar
4 eggs
230g plain flour
100g cocoa powder
½ tsp baking powder
2 tsp bicarbonate of soda

Preheat the oven to 180°C, butter and line a 23cm springform tin.

Pour the Guinness into a pan and heat, add the chocolate and allow to melt.

Beat the sugar and butter until light and fluffy.

Gradually add the eggs, then the dry ingredients. Pour the Guinness and melted chocolate into the mixture making sure you incorporate all the flour or you will have little white bits in your black cake.

Pour into a parchment lined tin. We use loaf tins so the cake comes out rectangular.

Bake at 160°C for 30–35 mins.

Crème caramel

serves 6

2 eggs
4 egg yolks
500ml full fat milk
100g caster or granulated sugar
vanilla essence/pod
pinch of salt

To make the caramel, gently melt 200g of caster or granulated sugar in a heavy based pan, swirling rather than stirring it to blend. When it is a uniform golden brown, remove from the heat and add a tablespoon of water, standing well back as it will spit initially. Once it has settled down and become smooth again, pour small amounts into individual dariole moulds and set aside.

Next make the custard.

Dariole moulds, mentioned below, are like little aluminium pudding basins, and very useful if you like making this pudding or are also good for pannacotta. You can of course make this in a large Pyrex dish but it will take longer to cook.

Bring the milk to boiling point. If using a vanilla pod, boil with the milk, then remove it, slice down the length of the pod and run the blade of a knife down the inside to remove the seeds. Add these to the egg mix.

Mix eggs, yolks, sugar, vanilla (essence or seeds) and salt and pour on hot milk. Pour into a jug.

Pour into the dariole moulds, and put into a roasting tin.

Set this onto the centre shelf of the oven and gradually fill with warm water until the moulds are about to float off.

Bake at 160ºC, but err on the side of caution as they do have a tendency to curdle if cooked too ferociously!

Once they have set (shake one and it should shiver very slightly), remove from the oven and from the roasting tin and allow to cool. To serve, run a knife round the outside and put a bowl or plate on the top, reverse the plate and mould and shake the crème caramel to release it, allowing the caramel to run down the pudding and make an alluring puddle on the plate.

puddings

Carrot cake

This recipe came from a lovely lady called Christine whose kids used to go to swimming galas with our boys when they were a lot younger. I always remember being surprised that it had oil in it.

Don't skimp on the frosting, it's a vital part of the whole carrot cake experience!

serves 6

3 eggs
50g caster sugar
250ml vegetable oil
1 handful chopped pecans
2 handfuls grated carrot
150g wholemeal flour
1 tsp mixed spice
1 tsp baking powder

Select 2 large mixing bowls.

Into one put the eggs, oil and carrots. Into the other put the sugar, pecans, flour, spice and baking powder.

Mix the wet ingredients into the dry until well combined.

Pour into a greased, lined springform tin and bake at 170°C for 35–45 mins until firm in the middle. Your skewer should come out clean.

Allow to cool in the tin before turning out onto a wire rack.

frosting

100g cream cheese
50g butter
100g icing sugar
zest and half the juice of a small lemon

You must make the frosting Kathy's way, and in my opinion it's the best bit!

Sieve the icing sugar into the beaten cream cheese and butter, incorporate the lemon zest and juice.

Resist eating it before it gets on to the cake!

Chocolate fudge cake

serves 6

3 eggs	Melt the butter and chocolate over a pan of simmering water.
175g caster sugar	Mix the breadcrumbs with the ground almonds.
vanilla aroma	Whisk the eggs, sugar and vanilla to a slightly thickened creamy consistency, then gently fold in the almonds and breadcrumbs. Finally add the melted chocolate mix until it is all well incorporated and there are no pockets of dry ingredients.
100g dark chocolate	
100g butter	
50g ground almonds	
125g fresh breadcrumbs	Grease and line a springform tin and pour in the mixture.
	Bake for about an hour at 150°C.

pecan butterscotch sauce

75g butter	Melt the butter with the soft brown sugar and whipping cream until all are incorporated, it doesn't need to boil.
75g soft brown sugar	
30ml whipping cream	Throw in a handful of roasted, chopped pecans and pour the sauce over the fudge cake.
50g cocoa powder – optional	
2 tblsp roasted, chopped pecans	Alternatively sieve the cocoa powder into the mixture to create an unctuous chocolate sauce!

or our own classic chocolate sauce

serves 4–5

100g butter	Melt the butter and add the cocoa, drinking chocolate and Golden Syrup.
100g cocoa powder	
100g drinking chocolate	Bring to boil and make sure all the powder is mixed well in, then add a little whipping cream.
200g Golden Syrup	
125ml whipping cream	Don't overcook the chocolate mixture as it will turn into a very solid toffee and be of no use.
	Great served with vanilla ice cream.

Christmas pud

This will make about 4 or 5 puddings but they do keep for next year
or you can give them to friends!

400g self-raising flour
pinch salt
350g white breadcrumbs
350g butter
460g soft brown sugar
460g currants
920g raisins
110g candied peel
rind and juice of one orange
30g sliced almonds
1 large cooking apple, peeled and grated
1 tsp mixed spice
6 eggs
200ml beer (dark ale or stout)

Put all the fruit and nuts into a large bowl and soak overnight in the beer, orange rind and juice.

Cream the butter and sugar together, then gradually add the eggs and the flour. Now mix in the fruit and stir up well – make a wish!

Line a pudding basin with foil and greaseproof paper, leaving enough of both to seal the pudding in around the top.

Tie a piece of string around the ridge on the bowl. This will keep the foil on and act like a handle. Fill the bowl to about 5cm from the top to allow space for rising.

Sit the pudding basin on a trivet to avoid the basin sitting on the bottom of the saucepan. Fill the saucepan with hot water up to the level of the string on the pudding basin. Steam in a deep saucepan with a lid for 4 hours keeping an eye on the water levels.

Hazelnut meringue

200g roasted, skinned and chopped
hazelnuts
100g white chocolate, chopped
100g dark chocolate, chopped
5 egg whites
350g caster sugar
1/2 tsp mixed spice

Line two baking sheets with bakewell paper.

Whisk egg whites until stiff and gradually whisk in 240g of the caster sugar.

Add the spice and fold in 100g of the chopped nuts and all of the chocolate.

Make one circular shape on each prepared baking sheet with the meringue mix and bake at 100°C for 2–2½ hours.

Allow to cool. Alternatively, spoon the mixture into individual nest shapes and cook in the same way.

Praline

100g caster sugar
100g chopped hazelnuts

Make a praline by melting the remaining 110g caster sugar in a heavy based saucepan until caramel coloured and add the remaining 100g chopped hazelnuts. Pour this very hot mixture onto a baking tray and chill.

When it is cold, break off the solid nutty caramel and blitz in a food processor until it is like crunchy breadcrumbs.

Layer the meringue with the cream and the praline, or fill the basket with cream and sprinkle the praline over.

Ciaran Hanna's magic meringues

The boys in the kitchen are not what you would call natural pastry cooks, but after our pastry chef left to go on perpetual maternity, leave we all had to muck in and do our stint on that section.

I asked Ciaran to make some meringues one day and he came up with this great pudding.

makes 6–8

4 egg whites
200g caster sugar
100g pecan nuts
100g dark chocolate buttons

Whisk the egg whites to soft peaks, add half the sugar, keep beating and then add the rest of the sugar and beat to stiff peak. Fold in the nuts and chocolate. With two spoons form portion sized shapes on baking parchment or a baking sheet, or you can pipe the meringue into a circular pastry cutter to get a nice round shape. Bake for 1 hour at 120°C.

Allow to cool completely before attempting to remove from the baking paper otherwise you will leave half the meringue on the paper.

Serve with sweetened whipped cream, raspberries and strawberries or vanilla ice cream with chocolate sauce.

Pannacotta

serves 6

750ml whipping or double cream
250ml milk
240g caster sugar
5 leaves of gelatine
250ml flavouring – this is usually a fruit purée, such as passion fruit or raspberry, but adding fruit does affect the setting properties of the gelatine so add an extra leaf if adding flavouring.

Heat the cream, milk and sugar in a pan.

Melt the gelatine in cold water and then add to the heated cream to dissolve. Finally add your chosen flavour and pour into moulds or glasses. The benefit of glasses means you don't have to unmould, but they do look very enticing sitting quivering on a plate, so if you do use a mould, run it under a very hot tap, ensuring you don't wet the pannacotta.

Put a serving plate over the open end and coax out the pannacotta.

yoghurt and honey pannacotta

serves 4

125ml cream
400g yoghurt with honey
2 small leaves of gelatine [soak in cold water to soften]
2 tblsp of flavoursome honey

Put the cream into a saucepan with the honey and heat until nearly boiling. Remove from the heat and dissolve the gelatine in the hot milk.

In a bowl, combine the cream and the yoghurt and put into moulds to set for at least 4 hours in the fridge.

Sable pastry

This is **the** dessert pastry and like all good things it's hard to work but well worth the effort!

250g butter
250g icing sugar
2 large eggs
90ml whipping cream
650g plain flour

In the bowl of a mixer, cream butter and icing sugar, next add the eggs and finally the flour. Just run the machine until you have a smooth dough, i.e. not long!

Remove the mixture from the bowl, wrap in clingfilm and chill in the fridge for 1 hour. This pastry is a nightmare to work with but tastes brilliant. I usually roll it out between two pieces of baking parchment. Or just use lots of flour and always leave a lip of spare pastry around the edge of the flan case to allow for shrinkage. You can trim it after it is cooked to make it neat and tidy.

Pecan pie

4 eggs
360g soft brown sugar
400g golden syrup
pinch salt
1 tblsp brandy or bourbon
200g melted butter
2 dsp vanilla essence

Make the filling the day before.

Blend all the ingredients together and leave to mature, overnight at least .... something magical happens to this combination if it is left to age slightly!

Press the sable pastry into the flan tin and bake blind in a cool oven at about 150°C. Remove the baking beans after 10 mins and return the tin the the oven to finish cooking the base. The idea being to cook the pastry with very little colour.

Spread the base with pecans to cover, give the syrup mixture a good stir up with a whisk, then pour in the mixture over the nuts and bake at 150°C for 30–45 mins, keeping an eye on it.

puddings

130

Lemon tart

Requested by Barbara Flinn, a classic – this recipe came from Nico Ladenis of 3 star
Chez Nico fame – a great hero of mine. Sadly, I never ate in his restaurant.

serves 6

blind sable pastry base in a 20cm tart ring.

egg mixed with 2 yolks to glaze the base of the tart.

4 lemons

zest of 2 lemons finely grated

165g caster sugar

6 eggs

350ml double cream

icing sugar (to glaze top of the tart)

Line the tart ring with the sable pastry as thin as you can. Line with baking parchment and baking beans.

Bake in a preheated oven at 150°C for 20 mins, then remove the paper and beans, and bake until the pastry is golden.

Remove from the oven and glaze with the eggwash mixture. Put back in the oven for 2 mins to seal the base.

Make syrup with the lemon juice and sugar, then pour the syrup over the eggs and whisk.

Bring the cream to the boil and whisk into the mixture, sieve onto the finely grated lemon zest and skim any froth off the top.

Pour the cream mixture into the pastry case and bake in a preheated oven at 180°C for 40 mins.

Remove from the oven and allow to cool, then chill in the fridge until set.

Dust the tart with icing sugar and glaze with a blowtorch.

Vanilla ice cream

My love of ice cream goes back a long way.

It has always been a source of some amazement that we allow manufacturers to make it with all sorts of things other than milk. I was so keen to make my own that I brought back an old fashioned ice cream churn from the States to which you add salt and ice to the outside drum and put your mix into the inner one. We are a lot more hi-tech now, but that old drum made great ice cream.

makes about 1 litre ice cream

1 vanilla pod
500ml milk
200g caster sugar
500ml double cream
8 egg yolks
pinch of salt

Put the milk, cream and 100g sugar into a saucepan. Split the vanilla pod and scrape out the seeds. Put the seeds and pod in with the milk and cream. Slowly bring to the boil or it will boil over.

Whisk the egg yolks and the other 100g sugar. Once the cream mixture has boiled add a pinch of salt and whisk it into the egg mixture.

Put back on the heat and cook gently watching all the time until the custard coats the back of a spoon, then strain through a sieve.

Allow the mixture to cool and then freeze in an ice cream machine.

The salt enhances the vanilla flavour in case you were wondering.

This is a vanilla base and you can flavour it as you see fit.

Baked rice pudding

This was requested by David Cromie on the condition it had raisins in it.

It always amazes me that the rice can absorb all the milk.

serves 4

50g pudding rice
600ml full cream milk
1 vanilla pod
zest of 1 lemon
2 tblsp soft brown sugar
pinch of nutmeg
butter
50g raisins

Put all the ingredients into a deep pyrex dish and mix thoroughly. Dot the top with butter.

Bake in a deep roasting tray with water about half way up the dish for about 2 hours at 160°C.

Bread and butter pudding

When Nick's first opened, the business lunch was alive and well, and customers dining upstairs quickly caught on to the fact that they needed to order this pudding on their way in, otherwise the downstairs lot would eat it all up!

serves 4

250ml cream
3 eggs
85g sugar
1 tsp vanilla extract
pinch of salt
50g butter
8 slices sliced white loaf
60g raisins
apricot jam

Butter the bread and cut into triangles. Lay them in a row in a rectangular dish. Then sprinkle with raisins and add another layer of bread on top. Make a custard with the eggs, sugar, vanilla and cream. Whisk them all together with a pinch of salt and pour over the bread. Bake in a bain marie (a roasting tray with water halfway up the bread dish) until golden brown.

When the pudding is cooked, make a glaze by melting some apricot jam with a little water and brush it over the top of the pudding. Put back into the oven for 10 mins to glaze. Serve immediately.

variation

Use Barmbrack or pannatone instead of the white sliced bread – really decadent!

Zucotto

We used to make this pudding in Kilmood many years ago. I think we added the cherries to the original recipe as we felt it was not a great colour. We have an ex-Kilmood customer who still comes in and asks for it now and again.

50g blanched almonds
50g hazelnuts
50g glacé cherries finely chopped
1 lt whipping cream
75g icing sugar
100g cooking chocolate grated
1 packet trifle sponges should do but have a spare standing by!
1 bottle marsala al oevo
icing sugar and chocolate powder or cocoa for dusting

serves 6

Put hazelnuts into a hot oven and leave for 5 mins. Rub off the skins and chop coarsely with the almonds. Whip the cream with the sugar until very stiff. Fold in the chopped nuts, cherries, the grated chocolate and 1 tablespoonful of marsala.

Slice the trifle sponges down the centre to make them thinner. Pour some of the marsala into a bowl and soak each slice in the marsala – add more as you need. Don't skimp as it won't taste as good!

Line a round pudding mould with cling film then line the bowl with the sponge slices, leaving no spaces. Fill the bowl with the cream mixture right to the top then layer the remaining sponge slices on top to form a base. Cover the bowl and weight with a plate and put into the fridge for 3 hours plus.

To serve, turn out on to a flat plate. Mark out 6 equal triangles on the pudding and dust alternative trianges with icing and cocoa/chocolate powder, white brown.

Fudge

Hands up – we stole from the Presbyterian Women's Cookbook. I suppose in the interests of equality I will have to source a recipe from the Catholic Country Women's Association. In fact these books are great repositories of all our cultural cooking traditions and are quite often handed down from mother to daughter. Who hasn't rushed to the cake stall to buy one of big Aggies finest chocolate sponges before someone else snapped it up?

900g soft brown sugar	In a saucepan melt the butter, add the sugar and milk.
110g butter	Boil for 10 mins, add the condensed milk and boil for 15–20 mins more.
1 cup milk	Beat well before pouring into a greased swiss roll tin.
1 tin condensed milk	

An Italian sweetmeat

We use it as a petit four.

100g cherries glazed	Mince the fruit and nuts in a coarse mincer. Add the brandy, sprinkle a board with icing sugar and knead the mixture to a thick paste. Roll up into a small salami shape 300cm long and 40mm thick. Set in the fridge rolled in icing sugar then wrapped up in foil for several hours before use. It will keep for ages.
100g sultanas	
100g dried figs	
100g dried apricots	
100g stoned dates	
100g blanched almonds	
100g shelled walnuts	
2–3 tblsp brandy	
icing sugar	

Chocolate truffles

We make these for our petits fours plates and you can flavour them with all sorts of things like cointreau, passionfruit or raspberry purée.

A confectioner would call this a chocolate ganache mix.

150g dark chocolate – 75% cocoa solids
150ml double cream
25g unsalted butter
2 tblsp rum/brandy/Bushmills whiskey
1 level tblsp Greek yoghurt

Blitz up the chocolate in a food processor to make it easy to melt.

In a saucepan put the cream butter and rum/brandy bringing to a simmer. Next pour this mixture onto the chocolate in the food processor with the motor running and blend until smooth.

Next, add the yoghurt and blend again. Pour the mixture into a bowl and put into the fridge to set. It will take a few hours to thicken up.

You have 2 options:

1 The clean way is to fill a piping bag with the mixture and pipe out long lines of the mix onto a tray lined with baking parchment. Then set in the fridge for an hour after which you can cut into 3 or 4cm lengths and roll these in cocoa powder. Return to the fridge to deep cool.

2 The other way is to let it set and just roll the ganache mix into little balls and roll them in cocoa powder. Brings back those mud pie days!

For Kathy, without whom there would be no Nick's Warehouse,
Adam and Ben,
and my Mum, who believed in us

The Price family

Adam, Nick, Ben
and Kathy

Sylvia Price,
aka Granny/Mum

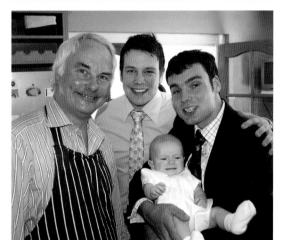

Three generations of
Prices – Nick, Ben,
Adam and Noah

Ben, Noah and Danielle

Sue and Brian

Published by Booklink, Ireland
120 High Street, Holywood BT18 9HW
Publisher: Dr. Claude Costecalde

www.nickswarehouse.co.uk

ISBN 978-1-906886-23-3

Design by Wendy Dunbar, Dunbar Design
Printed in Slovenia